A first course in typing

D. J. Thomas M.A., B.Sc.(Econ.), Ph.D.

Bell & Hyman

First published in 1982 by
BELL & HYMAN LIMITED
Denmark House
37–39 Queen Elizabeth Street
London SE1 2QB

British Library Cataloguing in Publication Data
Thomas, D.J.
A first course in typing.
1. Typewriting.
I. Title
652.3   Z49

ISBN 0 7135 1326 8

Typeset in Singapore by
Polyglot Pte Ltd.
Printed in Great Britain by
William Clowes, Beccles, Suffolk.

CONTENTS

One space

(1) Before and after the *ampersand*, e.g. Barnwell & Co Ltd.
(2) Before and after a *multiplication* sign, e.g. 10×14.
(3) Before and after a *minus* sign, e.g. $6 - 3$.
(4) Before and after a *division* sign, e.g. $40 \div 4$.
(5) Before and after a *plus* sign, e.g. $7 + 3$.
(6) Before and after an *equals* sign, e.g. $7 + 3 = 10$.
(7) Before and after the *at* sign, e.g. 7 @ £5 each.

APPENDIX IV

Care of the typewriter

A typewriter is an expensive machine and, as with most machines, a certain amount of attention is required to maintain it in good condition.

Cleaning

1 Dust should be removed regularly, using a soft, dry cloth. A long-handled soft brush, similar to a paintbrush, may be used to clean corners. In order to avoid dust settling, the machine should be kept covered when not in use.
2 The type should be brushed regularly, using a type-cleaning brush (which resembles a toothbrush). Occasionally it will be necessary to remove obstinate dirt by applying cleaning or methylated spirit.

Removal

Before a typewriter is moved the carriage should be locked by moving the left and right-margin stops to the centre of the carriage. This prevents the carriage sliding to left or right while the machine is being carried.

When the machine is lifted, the keys should be positioned away from the body. The hands should be placed under each side of the frame so that they take the full weight. It is easier to carry a typewriter held in this way and any possible damage to the keys is avoided.

The Ribbon

The ribbon is wound automatically between two spools. When the ribbon produces only faint impressions it has worn out and must be replaced. It should be noted that many makes of machine have their own special ribbon spools, which will not fit machines of other makes.

Backing Sheet

Wear on the platen is reduced by using an extra sheet of paper behind the one being typed. This also ensures a better impression.

A note on examinations

1 Read through the question paper before starting to type.
2 Read carefully the instructions for each question. Failure to follow instructions in answering questions is a major cause of failure in typewriting examinations.
3 Be consistent in answers. For example, if a date is typed first as 8 December 19——, it must be typed in the same way (e.g. *not* December 8 19——) if occurring again.
4 Do not mix styles, such as blocked or centred display.
5 Check an answer before the paper is taken out of the machine.
6 Correct neatly any typing errors. *Never* overtype.

APPENDIX I

Rules for division of words

Divide words
1 Between syllables, e.g. micro-scope, con-tain.
2 Between consonants, e.g. let-ter, neces-sary.
3 After a prefix, e.g. un-able, dis-appoint.
4 Before a suffix, e.g. harm-less, help-ful.
5 Where a hyphen occurs, e.g. self-confidence, well-off.

Do not divide
1 Words of one syllable or their plurals, e.g. piece, pieces.
2 Where only 2 letters remain for the next line, e.g. er, ly.
3 Words of 4 letters, e.g. upon, into.
4 Proper names, e.g. William, Tuesday, Leeds.
5 Number and sums of money, e.g. 7,940, £24.70.
6 The last word in a paragraph or on a page.
7 Abbreviations or contractions, e.g. COD, DSc.
8 Dates.

APPENDIX II

Spacing after punctuation

No space
(1) Before or after a *hyphen*, e.g. half-term or an *apostrophe* when it comes before the s, e.g. John's book.
(2) After an *opening bracket* or before a *closing bracket*, e.g. That house (number 214) is old.
(3) After an *opening quotation mark* or before a *closing quotation mark*, e.g. 'Go at once.'
(4) Before or after a *full stop* used as a decimal point, e.g. £20.10

One space
(1) After a *comma*, *colon* or *semicolon*.
(2) After an *apostrophe* when it comes after the s. E.g. Three months' notice is required.
(3) Before and after the *hyphen* used as a dash, e.g. She will arrive soon – at least, I hope so.

Two spaces
After a *full stop*, an *exclamation mark* or a *question mark* at the end of a sentence.

APPENDIX III

Spacing after miscellaneous characters

No space
(1) Before the % symbol, e.g. $10\frac{1}{2}\%$ interest.
(2) Before or after the solidus sign, e.g. Ask him/her to go.
(3) After the £ sign, e.g. £45.
(4) Between figures and letter p when typing sums of money, e.g. 85p

LIST OF DIAGRAMS IN THE TEXT

1 Clear all tab stops.

2 Turn up two single-line spaces before the part of the letter to be displayed.

3 Select the longest line in the *first* column and starting from the left-hand margin, tap the space bar once for each character and space (8).

4 Add the number of spaces (e.g. 3) to be left between the longest line of the first column and the start of the second column and set a tab stop at the point reached.

5 Select the longest line in the *second* column and tap the space bar once for each character and space plus the three spaces between the second and third columns (30). Set a tab stop at this point.

6 Type the display section.

7 Turn up two single-line spaces after the display section.

```
Ref NS/LM


20 March 19--


School Books Ltd
77 Learning Way
BIRMINGHAM
BR2 3AM

For the attention of Mr A Binder

Dear Sirs

I would be grateful if you would send a quotation for the
supply of the following.

100          Account Journals      No JO/2
10 dozen     Wallet Files          No LE/3
5 gross      Blue Exercise Books   No CA/56

We require these items for the start of the autumn term in
September and should like you to indicate a delivery date.

I should appreciate a copy of your latest stationery
catalogue.

Yours faithfully



N Smith
Head of Commerce Department
```

QUESTIONS

Write short answers to the following.

1 Give four ways in which information may be displayed in a letter.

2 How many spaces are used to separate displayed matter from the rest of the letter?

PREFACE

Typewriting can be a valuable personal skill to everyone. The aim of this volume is to provide a textbook on typewriting suitable for secondary school courses leading to the Certificate of Secondary Education. It is designed also for students taking the elementary typewriting examinations of the Royal Society of Arts; the Pitman Examinations Institute; and the London Chamber of Commerce. In addition, the book is suitable for the typewriting module in the Business and Technician Education Council (BTEC) General Award Courses.

Included within the book are questions requiring short answers and questions from recent C.S.E. and other public examination papers.

I wish to record my gratitude to Miss M S Lawrence for much helpful advice and for time given to checking and typing the manuscript.

I wish to thank the London Regional Examinations Board (L.R.E.B.), the Yorkshire Regional Examinations Board (Y.R.E.B.), the West Midlands Examinations Board (W.M.E.B.), the Welsh Joint Education Committee (W.J.E.C.), the West Yorkshire and Lindsey Regional Examining Board (W.Y. & L.R.E.B.), the Associated Lancashire Schools Examining Board (A.L.S.E.B.), the South Western Examinations Board (S.W.E.B.), the North West Regional Examination Board (N.W.R.E.B.), the London Chamber of Commerce (L.C.C.) and the Royal Society of Arts (R.S.A.) who have permitted the reproduction of questions taken from previous examination papers.

D. J. T.

INTRODUCTION

A typewriter is a writing machine which performs the work of writing at a speed far greater than is possible with a pen. The machine is operated by means of a keyboard and produces characters similar to those used in printing.

Records show that the first attempts to produce a typewriter were made early in the eighteenth century. However, it was not until 1874 that a machine capable of writing faster than a pen and which could be manufactured by mass production methods at a reasonable price was produced. This first practical typewriter was invented by three Americans—Christopher Latham Sholes, Carlos Glidden and Samuel W. Soulé.

Early in this century the first portable typewriters were introduced, and by 1920 a working model of an electric typewriter (that is, a machine with the typing stroke powered by an electric motor drive) had been produced.

In recent years, an automatic word processing typewriter has been introduced. The machine has an electronic *memory* which automatically stores everything that is typed. Material can be *recalled* (and corrected or altered if necessary) and then reproduced at high speeds.

Exercise 2

Type this letter in fully blocked style on A4 paper (210 × 297 mm) and make one carbon copy. Insert today's date. Type an envelope for the letter.

Turn up 13 single lines from the top of A4 paper to represent the printed name and address of an organisation.

Set margins at 12–72 (pica) or 22–82 (elite) for the first and last paragraphs and 12–60 (pica) and 22–70 (elite) for the displayed part.

Our Ref SO/MT

Mr L C James
12 Cedars Road
BIRMINGTON
BR9 6ON

Dear Mr James

Thank you for your recent letter. We have pleasure in listing below the details of a property in the locality mentioned in your letter.

THE ELMS, TREEVILLE - built 1979
Semi-detached house with large rear garden, garage and space for caravan or boat.
Lounge, dining room, modernised kitchen.
Three bedrooms, bathroom with shower, separate toilet.
Gas-fired central heating.
Outside: greenhouse and garden shed.
Price: £37 500

We shall be pleased to make an appointment to view at a time convenient to you.
Yours sincerely
SELLWELL & CO LTD

(space)
(SALES EXECUTIVE)

Exercise 3

Type the following letter on A4 paper (210 × 297 mm) in fully blocked style. Margins are set at 12–72 (pica) or 22–82 (elite). Turn up 13 lines from the top of the paper to represent the printed name and address of an organisation.

Note In fully blocked letters all lines start at the left-hand margin. When the information to be displayed is in columnar form (as in this exercise) the following steps are required.

I UNDERSTANDING THE TYPEWRITER

1 Parts of the typewriter

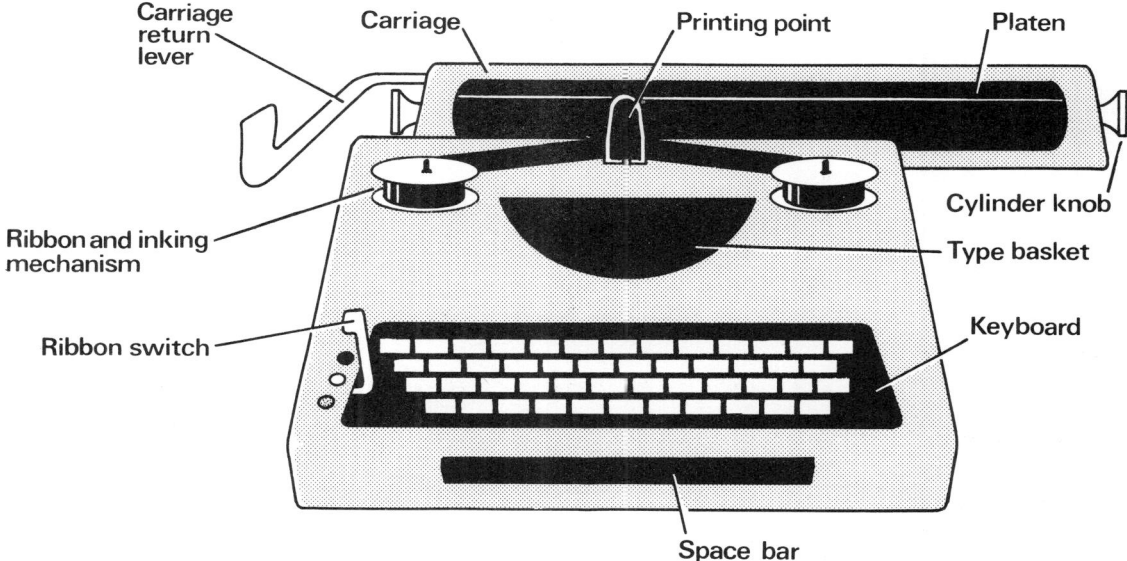

Fig. 1 Components of the typewriter

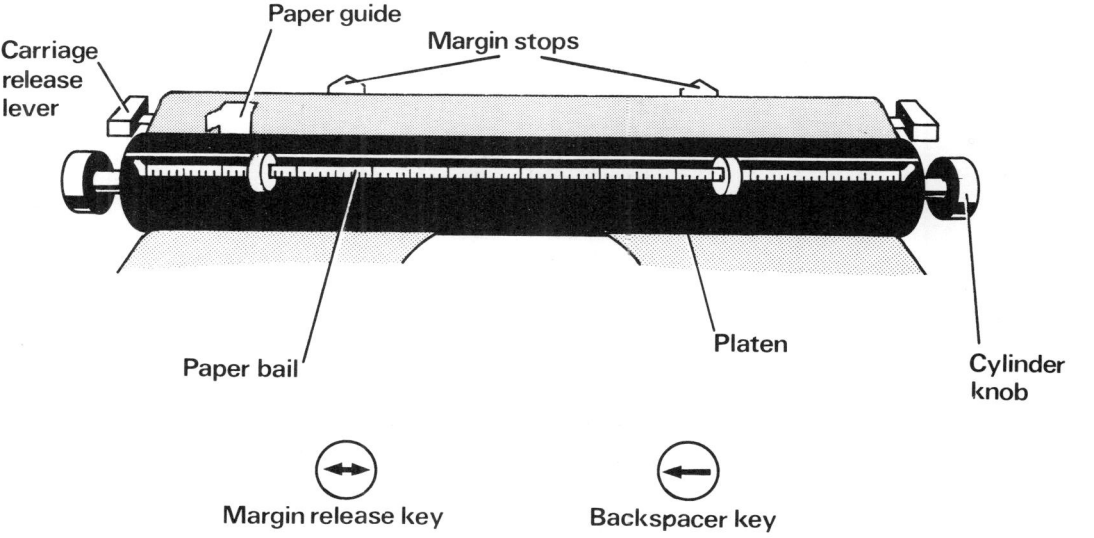

Fig. 2 The carriage

Note   Displayed matter is separated from the rest of the letter by one clear space above and below.

Our Ref JB/ST

4 May 19--

A Buyer Esq
14 The View
PRIMTOWN
PR3 6WN

Dear Sir

We thank you for your letter requesting details of properties which we are offering for sale in the Silvermead area of this city. Brief details are given below of two properties which might be suitable:

SILVER STAR DRIVE A four bedroom detached house with lounge, dining room, kitchen, bathroom and garaging for two cars. Mature gardens back and front. Close to shops and other amenities. Rateable value £756. Freehold.

SILVER GLOW AVENUE A ground floor flat with three bedrooms, lounge, dining room and kitchen. Electric underfloor heating. Situated in small block of twelve flats surrounded by landscaped grounds. Garage available. Rateable value £593. Leasehold.

If you would like to inspect these properties, we should be pleased to make the necessary arrangements.

Yours faithfully
JOYFUL ESTATES LTD

Sales Director

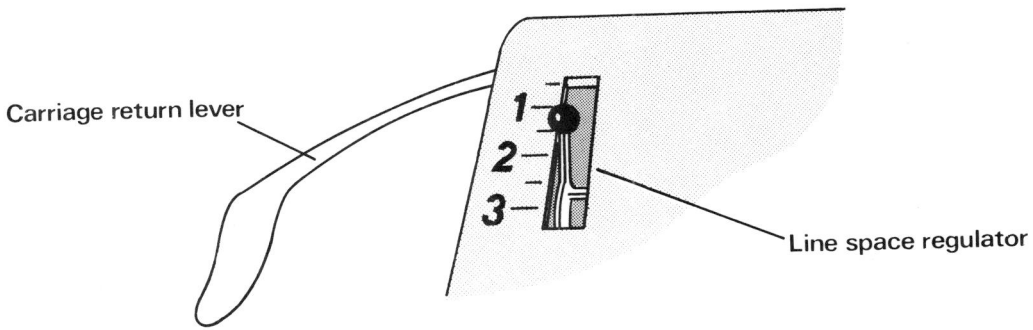

Fig. 3 Carriage return lever and line-space regulator

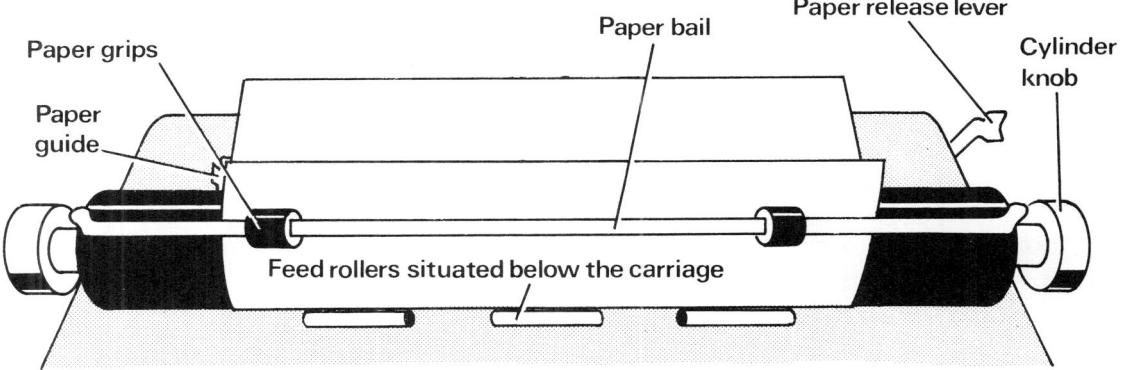

Fig. 4 Paper holding and releasing

The most important parts of the typewriter are identified in the list given below. The exact location of a part may differ, due to variations in the construction of different makes of machine.

Platen: a cylinder around which the paper is held in position. The *cylinder knobs* are turned for the insertion and removal of the paper. (Fig. 2)

Carriage release lever: the lever which frees the carriage so that it can be moved easily to the left and right. (Fig. 2)

Back spacer: a key which is used to move the carriage back one space at a time. (Fig. 2)

Carriage return lever: this lever is used for returning the carriage to the right in order to begin a new line. It is also used for turning up the paper when desired. (Fig. 3)

Line space regulator: the regulator controls the distance that the paper turns up when the carriage is returned. The gauge may be set for single-, double- or treble-line spacing (with half-line spacing on some machines). (Fig. 3 and Fig. 5)

Exercise 8
Details for completion of Exercise 7:

Our Ref. is The Manager's initials/Typist's initials. Date letter as for today.

To: Mr S O Slocombe   93 The Haven Wolton Staffs.
   Lake Lugano   Italy.
   The Italian State Office, 201 Regent Street, London W1.
   01–734–2818

QUESTIONS
Write short answers to the following.
1   What is a form letter?
2   State briefly how the use of form letters saves typing time.
3   Give three examples of the use of form letters.

37 Displayed letters
When it is desirable to place emphasis on particular information within a letter, it may be displayed in a variety of ways. For example:
1   line spacing may be varied,
2   different margins may be used,
3   the items or paragraphs may be numbered (see chapter 25),
4   the information may be arranged in columns (see chapter 27).

EXERCISES

Exercise 1
Type the following fully-blocked letter on A4 paper (210 × 297 mm). Set margins at 12–72 (pica) or 22–82 (elite) for the first and last paragraphs and 12–60 (pica) or 22–70 (elite) for the middle part. Turn up 13 single lines from the top of A4 paper to represent the printed name and address of an organisation.

Single-line spacing

    When the line space regulator is set on 1, there is
type on every line. The lines are clearly separated, but
there is not a full line of space between the lines of type.

Double-line spacing

    When the line space regulator is set on 2, there is
                    (One single blank line)
type on every second line. There is one full line of space
                    (One single blank line)
between the lines of type.

Treble-line spacing

    When the line space regulator is set on 3, there is
                    (One single blank line)
                    (One single blank line)
type on every third line. There are two full lines of
                    (One single blank line)
                    (One single blank line)
spaces between the lines of type.

Fig. 5 Single-, double-, and treble-line spacing

Feed rollers: these small rubber rollers grip the paper in position. (Fig. 4)

Paper grips: a set of small rollers which hold the paper firmly against the platen. They are mounted on the *paper bail* which must be raised or pulled forward when the paper is inserted or removed. (Fig. 4)

Paper release lever: this lever is used to move the feed rollers away from the platen thus releasing the paper for adjustment or removal from the machine. (Fig. 4)

Paper guide: a guide used to position the left-hand edge of the paper as it is inserted in the machine. (Fig. 4)

Margin stops: these stops are used to fix the points at which the lines of typewriting begin on the left and end on the right. A *bell* rings to warn the typist when the carriage is nearing the end of the line. (Fig. 2)

Margin release key: depression of this key permits typing beyond the set margin points at either end of the line. (Fig. 2)

Exercise 7

Type the form below on A4 paper (210 × 297 mm), margins 10–72 (pica) 15–85 (elite), and then complete the details (supplied overleaf).

```
                    UNIVERSAL TRAVEL AGENTS LTD
                        3 Nelson Buildings
                         Trafalgar Square
                        London   WC2B 5PB

Manager: E D Whitehouse                    Tel: 01-405-4481


Our Ref


_____

_____

_____

_____


Dear _____

Thank you for your recent enquiry.  I have pleasure in

giving you the following details of holidays in _____

Full details are given in the colour brochures enclosed.

Further information about the region you propose to visit

can be obtained from:  _____

                       _____

                       _____

                       _____

                    Telephone No  _____

I hope to have the pleasure of making your holiday

arrangements for you.

Yours sincerely



Manager


Enc
```

2 Preparing to type

Typewriting paper sizes

The standard sizes are known as the A series and are shown below. (Fig. 6)

The two sizes of paper most commonly used are A4 and A5. Long letters are typed on A4 paper, and short letters on A5.

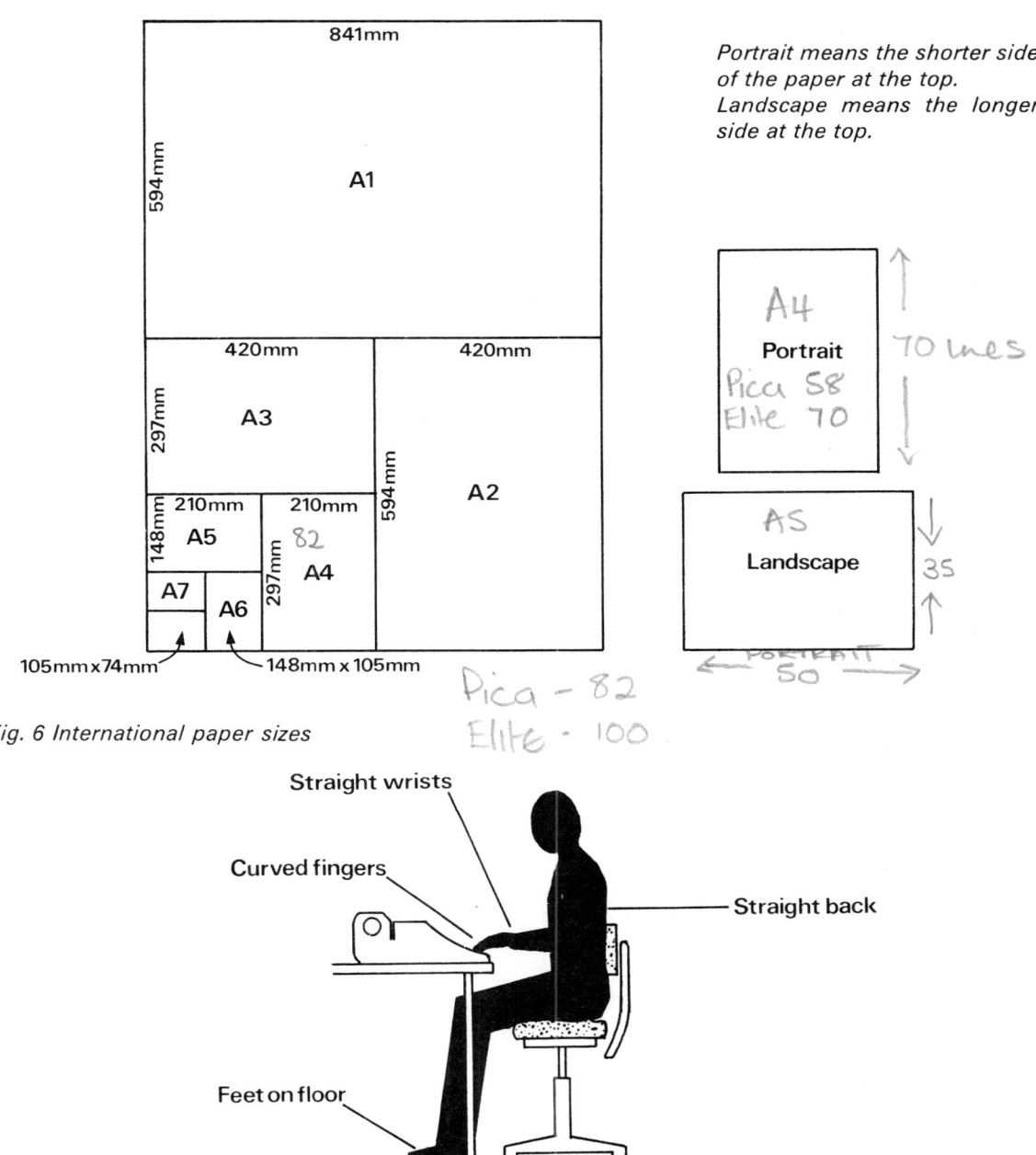

Portrait means the shorter side of the paper at the top.
Landscape means the longer side at the top.

Fig. 6 International paper sizes

Fig. 7 Position at the machine

Reference: NR/MSL

Date: Today's

To: Dr V Smooth Headmaster Primrose Path Secondary School

     Woodland Way GREENTOWN GR2 9WN

Re: Miss Susan Gargle - the position of Assistant Teacher

Exercise 5
Use the original of the form letter prepared in Exercise 3 on page 184 and insert the following details.

Reference: AJ/AMK

Date: Today's

To: Mr I Box 34 Crystal Street FREEZEVILLE FR1 3LE

Appointment: 14 March at 10 am

Exercise 6
Complete the form letter prepared in Exercise 2 on page 183 with the following details and date for despatch 5 days after date of enquiry.

Reference: FC 17982

Subject heading: Automatic Dictating Machines

Enquiry dated 12 May, 19__.

Price guaranteed for 21 days

RSL 37981	Dictation/Transcription Machine	£	118.80
RSL 37982	Microphone	£	17.47
RSL 37984	Stethoscope Headphones	£	12.35
RSL 37987	Foot Control	£	9.85
RSL 37989	Carrying Case	£	10.95

Position at the machine

Figure 7 suggests ways of obtaining a comfortable sitting position. The height of the table and chair should be adjusted so that a natural and easy position can be adopted.

The typewriting table should be in a good light and positioned so that shadows do not fall on the copy.

The copy is best placed either behind or on the right-hand side of the machine in order that operation of the carriage return lever does not obstruct the vision.

Type sizes

The two most usual type faces are *pica* and *elite*. (Fig. 8) Both pica and elite machines give six lines of type to every inch (25 mm) down a sheet of paper.

```
Pica type has 10 letters to the inch (25 mm).

Elite type has 12 letters to the inch (25 mm).
```

Fig. 8 Line of elite type and line of pica type

Touch typewriting

The aim should be to type by touch rather than looking at the keys. A great deal of time is saved by keeping the eyes fixed on the copy. In addition the possibility of mistakes which can arise when the attention switches between the copy and the machine (e.g. the omission of words or the repetition of words) is avoided.

Striking the keys

The keys should be struck as lightly but sharply as possible. The aim is to make the key strike the ribbon through its own momentum and so keys must not be pushed or pressed. Every attempt must be made to strike the keys evenly.

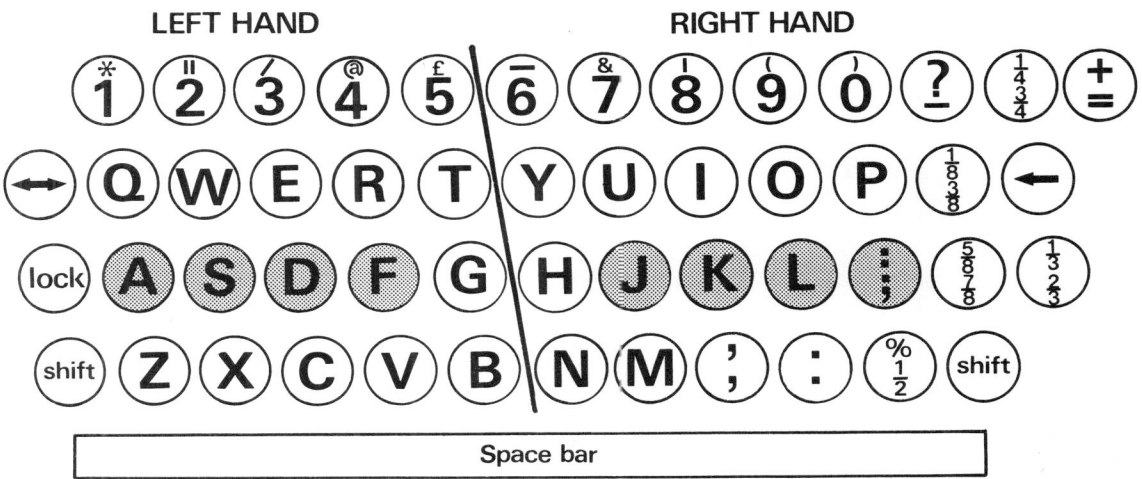

Fig. 9 The keyboard

Exercise 3

Type the example of a form letter in fully blocked style and take one carbon copy. Use A5 portrait paper (148 × 210 mm) and type in double-line spacing. Set margins at 5–55 (pica) or 12–62 (elite). Allow 9 single-line spaces down from the top of the paper to represent the printed name and address of an organisation.

```
Our Ref


Date:




Dear

An appointment has been made for our engineer to

call and service your gas central heating boiler

on        at      .  If this arrangement is not

convenient, will you please telephone us as soon

as possible.

Yours faithfully
MENDWELL LTD
```

Completion of a form letter

Care is required to ensure that the details fit into the correct position on the form letter.

In order to achieve this the margins must be carefully adjusted (use the same margins for preparation of the letter) and the line spacing regulated. The interliner and paper release lever are used to ensure that the material is correctly aligned.

Note that one space is left after the last character before starting to insert material.

Exercise 4

Use the original of the form letter prepared in Exercise 1 on page 182 and insert the following details.

The keyboard

A standard arrangement for the keyboard has been developed by typewriter manufacturers. The alphabetical letters are arranged in three rows as shown in Fig. 9. This standardisation of keyboards enables a typist to operate any machine produced by the leading typewriter manufacturers.

Figure 9 also shows that, for learning purposes, the keyboard is divided into two parts – right and left – and each hand is used for its own side of the keyboard only.

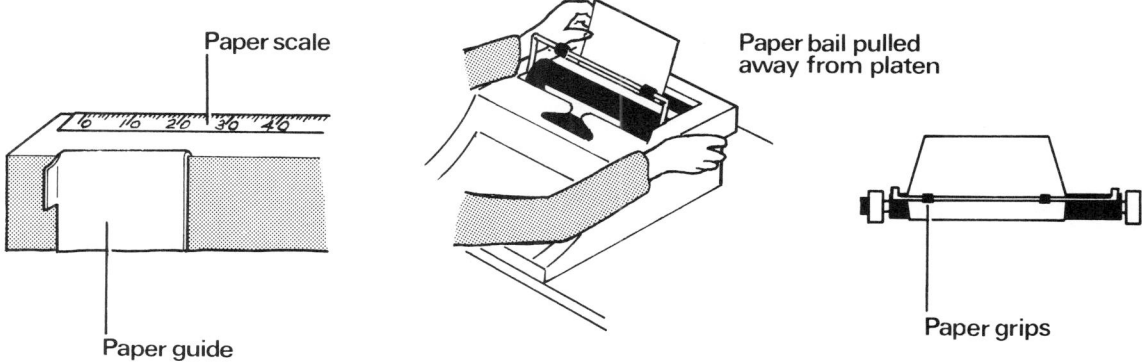

Fig. 10 Paper insertion and removal

Paper insertion and removal

1 Pull paper bail away from the platen.

2 Using the left hand place the paper behind the platen and against the raised edge of the paper guide set at 0 on the paper guide scale.

3 Turn the right-hand cylinder knob to draw the paper into the machine. (Fig. 10)

4 If the paper has not fed in evenly, it can be adjusted by using the paper release lever.

5 Set the paper bail back so that the paper grips hold the paper firmly against the platen.

The paper can be withdrawn by pulling lightly at the top left-hand corner at the same time as the paper release lever is operated. The paper must not be ripped out of the machine otherwise the feed rollers will suffer premature wear and cause the paper to slip.

Setting margins

The following table may be useful when working through exercises for learning the keyboard.

A4 paper (210 x 297 mm)

	pica type	elite type
For a typing line of 40 spaces set margins at	22–62	30–70
" " " " " 50 " " " "	18–68	25–75
" " " " " 60 " " " "	12–72	20–80

Exercise 2

Type the example of a form letter in fully blocked style. Use A4 paper (210 × 297 mm) and type in double-line spacing. Set margins at 12–72 (pica) or 22–82 (elite). Allow 12 single-line spaces from the top of the paper to represent the printed name and address of an organisation.

```
Reference  ....................

Date  ........................

Dear Customer

...............................

Thank you for your enquiry dated  ........................

The prices of the items you requested are given below.   These

apply only to present stock and so we are therefore unable

to guarantee them for a period longer than  ................

days from the date of this letter.

Yours faithfully

P J Mortimer

Sales Manager
```

Catalogue Number	Description of Items	Price Excluding VAT

II LEARNING THE KEYBOARD

3 The second row of keys

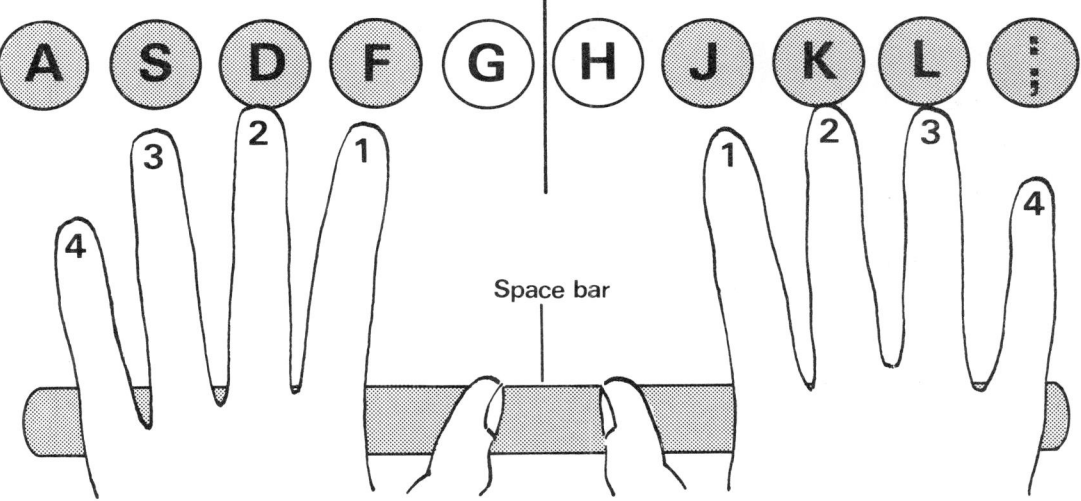

Fig. 11 *The second row of keys: the guide keys*

The second row of keys from the space bar contains the *guide* (or *home* keys). The guide keys are of particular importance because the four fingers of each hand rest over these keys and must return there after striking any other key. Figure 11 shows the correct position of the fingers on the guide keys: ASDF JKL;

The space bar should always be struck with the right-hand thumb.

EXERCISES
It is recommended that each line should be typed at least three times.

Typing line: 40 spaces. Single-line spacing.

Keys J and F

1   jj ff jj ff jf jf fj fj jj fjf jffj fjjf

Keys K and D

2   kk dd kk dd kd kd dk dk dd kdk dkkd kddk

3   kj jk kjk jkj jkf fkj kjf kfjk jkfj kjfk

4   df fd dfd fdf fdk dfk kdf dkfd djkd fkdk

5   dfj kdj fkd jdf fdk jjd jfd kdf jfj dfjd

(Turn up 4 lines)

Churchfold High School
Scholar Way
West Bromwich
WE3 20L

(Turn up 3 lines)

Ref

(Turn up 3 lines)

Date

(Turn up 10 lines)

Dear
(Turn up 2 lines)
Re:
(Turn up 2 lines)
The above named has applied to me for the position
of   *(Leave 19 spaces)*   and has given your name as
referee.

I would be grateful if you would advise me, in
confidence, as to his/her suitability for this
post.

Yours faithfully

(Turn up 5 lines)

N Rough
Headteacher

Fig. 34 A form letter

182

Keys L and S

6   ll ss ll ss ls ls sl sl ll sls lssl slls

7   lsj slf ksl sdl sfs lfl dss ksj llf slsl

8   slk lsj dlk fls jlk fks sls skf jks dlsd

9   sld lsd lkd sjl sjfd jldf klsf dssl dlsk

Keys ; and A

10   ;; aa ;; aa ;a ;a a; a; ;; a;a a;a; a;a;

11   jak alk laj kla ajk asd daf sad dal fla;

12   lad; sad; ask; lad; ask; sad; all; lass;

13   dad; fad; ass; add; dad; dad; all; fall;

Using the guide keys

14   asdf jkl; asdf jkl; fdsa ;lkj fdsa ;lkj;

15   sfad lj;k sfad lj;k sadf l;kf sadf l;kf;

16   all alas asks adds falls lass lads; dad;

17   a sad dad; a lass asks; alas a lad falls

18   ask a dad; a lad falls; a lass asks dad;

Keys H and G
The J finger is used to strike H; and the F finger is used for G. (Fig. 11)

19   jj hh jj hh jh jh hj hj jj hjh jhhj hjjh

20   ff gg ff gg fg fg gf gf ff gfg fggf gffg

21   jhf hjg jhg hjf fgjh gfhj fghj gfjh fgfj

22   has glad glass flag gall sash dash shall

QUESTIONS

Write short answers to the following.
1 What are circular letters?
2 Give two examples of the use of circular letters.
3 Describe a popular method of producing circular letters.
4 When a circular letter has a tear-off portion at the end, it is separated from the letter by a line of continuous _____ .

36 Form letters

A form letter is a term used to describe duplicated letters, printed forms or postcards which contain a standard form of wording. When a form letter is used, the typist has only to select the one appropriate to the circumstances, fill in the date, name and address of the addressee, and insert a few details in the body of the letter. Thus there is a saving in typing time.

Form letters may be used in a variety of ways, e.g. to acknowledge receipt of a communication, to provide notice of a medical appointment, and to inform a borrower from a public library of the availability of a book.

Preparation of a form letter

EXERCISES

Exercise 1

Type the example of a form letter (Fig. 34 overleaf) in fully blocked style and take one carbon copy. Use A5 portrait paper (148 × 210 mm) and type in single-line spacing. Set margins at 5–55 (piça) or 12–62 (elite).

Note (1) Adequate space between the date and the salutation must be allowed for insertion of the name and address of the addressee.

(2) Spaces must be left as indicated for filling in the appropriate details.

Using the second row of keys

23 gas sag ash has jag gas sag ash has jag;

24 glad dash half gall glad dash half gall;

25 salad; glass; flask; salad; glass; flask

26 alas a gala flag falls; a flash as glass

27 a glass flask; dad has had a fall; alas;

4 The third row of keys

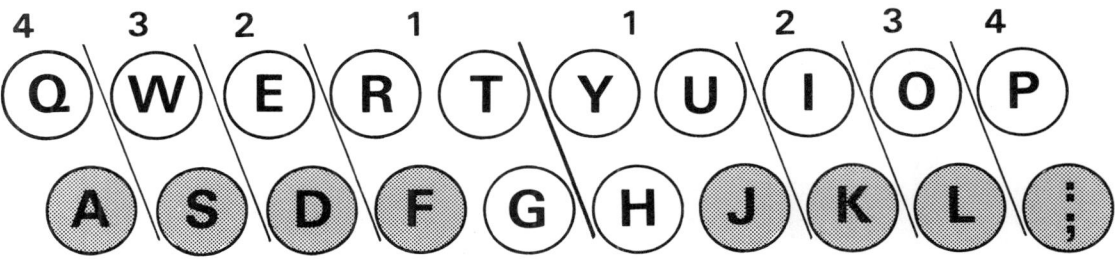

Fig. 12 The third row of keys

Figure 12 shows the fingers (as numbers) to be used for reaching from the guide keys to the third row.

When a key in the third row is struck the aim should be to move only the operating finger upwards. The other fingers should keep to their guide key positions.

EXERCISES

It is recommended that each line should be typed at least three times.

Typing line: 40 spaces. Single-line spacing.

Keys T and R

1 ff tt ff tt ft ft tf tf ff tft fttf tfft

2 ff rr ff rr fr fr rf rf ff rfr frrf rffr

3 jtf ktf dtf ltf stf fast flat last stall

4 jrf krf drf lrf srf jar far tar rag rats

5 sat fat tall rags; task last flats talk;

6 a tall lass has a flat hat; a stall jar;

15

Exercise 3
Type on A4 paper.

```
F O R E S T    V A L E    N U R S E R Y     Barton Lane
                                            Abbeyfield
                                            Cumbria
                                            AY4 6VW

BORDER PLANNING SERVICE

A new service available to customers within a 30-mile
radius of Forest Vale Nursery.

We will plan your border

Draw an outline sketch on a separate sheet, giving
dimensions of the area and indicating North and South.

Complete the form below and send this with your sketch.

The charge for this service is from £5.00 to
£10.00 according to the work involved.

Allow up to three weeks for the preparation of the
plan.
```

```
QUESTIONNAIRE

Give the nature of the soil.


Is the soil acid, limey or neutral?  Are rhododendrons
growing in your garden?


What is the surrounding vegetation?



List the shrubs you would like to be included.



NAME .....................................
ADDRESS .................................
        .................................
        .................................
```

180

Keys Y and U

7   jj yy jj yy jy jy yj yj jj yjy jyyj yjjy

8   jj uu jj uu ju ju uj uj jj uju juuj ujju

9   jyj kyj dyf ayj lyf syf sty say ray gray

10 juf kuf duf luf suf hug jugs rush dulls;

11 rug tug stay tray stray stuff rust trust

12 a dull day; dad has a jug; a rusty tray;

Keys I and E

13 kk ii kk ii ki ki ik ik kk iki kiik ikki

14 dd ee dd ee ed ed de de dd ede deed edde

15 rig fig his ill dig jig fit sit till it;

16 ear the jet key eat set yet eye let feet

17 rate rail trial seed feet site rest fear

18 the kite flies; eat the figs; wait here;

Using keys TRYUIE

19 fttf frrf jyyj juuj kiik deed rtyu iety;

20 they are at the sea; ask if he has a key

21 ask after her; try three jaffas; she is;

22 get a kite; she garages it at this date;

23 dad tried a full glass at the hut there;

24 he has hired a flat; she is at the lake;

25 that day they tried a salad; take a hat;

26 take a large glass; he has the red tray;

Exercise 2

Copy this example of a circular letter in single-line spacing. Use A4 paper (210 × 297 mm). Set margins: 22–82 (elite), 12–72 (pica).

```
AG/AN


Date as Postmark


Dear Member

We hope to hold our Autumn Fair on Saturday 1 October.  If
you are able to help in any way we shall be most grateful.
If you can give any of your time and/or items for any
stall(s) will you please fill in the Attached Slip and
return it to me as soon as possible?

In previous years the Fair has been very successful and both
the Club and various Local Charities have benefited from it.
As before admission will be by programme and each programme
will carry a lucky number.  "Lucky Number" gifts will be on
show in shops selling programmes.

Yours sincerely



Alf Glee
Social Secretary
```

```
Autumn Fair

Name ................................. Tel. No. ..........

Address ...................................................

I am willing to help sell programmes*
                     organise sports*
                     in any other way *
                     by providing items for (name stall)*

                                          ............

Signature ...................

*Please delete items which do not apply.
```

27 let her rest; they are at the little hut

28 the red rug is here; shut the tall gates

29 they are still here; their father is ill

30 a jet left the airfield early yesterday;

Keys O and W

31 ll oo ll oo lo lo ol ol ll olo lool ollo

32 ss ww ss ww sw sw ws ws ss wsw swws wssw

33 old too got lot food soot foot tool root

34 dew few sew row wood wild wool west wake

35 he always throws away the old white wool

36 it is too hot to eat a lot of food today

37 we will sow a few of the old wheat seeds

38 we would all like to go through the wood

Keys P and Q

39 ;; pp ;; pp ;p ;p p; p; ;; ;p; ;pp; p;;p

40 aa qq aa qq aq aq qa qa aa qaq aqqa qaaq

41 pot sip top pip pass post stop slap step

42 equal quite quest quake quay queue quail

43 it is quite a pretty pot; a steep slope;

44 please persuade her to stop at the quay;

45 those fresh apple pies looked pretty hot

46 do ask the poor people to queue quietly;

(Turn up 13 lines)

SAR/WL

(Turn up 3 lines)

Date as Postmark

(Turn up 3 lines)

Dear Parent

(Turn up 2 lines)

As the beginning of the new school year is also the start of a new period of office for Governing Bodies, it is necessary to make arrangements for the election of representatives of the parents to be co-opted on to the Governing Body of the school. It is in this connection that I am writing on behalf of the Chairman, Mrs O Henn, to invite you to attend a parents' meeting on Thursday, 29 September, at 7 30 pm in the School Hall.

The Governing Body of the school is comprised of three representatives of the Education Committee; one assistant teacher in the school; four co-opted members representing the interests of the local community, two of whom shall be parents of children attending the school. The Parent-Governors are to be chosen democratically at a meeting of all parents. Nominations for election will be accepted at the meeting.

It will be helpful for me to know whether or not you are able to attend on the evening in question and I shall be grateful if you will complete and return the tear-off slip below.

Yours sincerely

(Turn up 5 lines)

S A Rockman
Headmaster

(Turn up 2 lines)

(Turn up 3 lines)

Parents' Meeting, Thursday 29 September at 7 30 pm

Name ....

Address ....

I shall/shall not be present.

Fig. 33 A circular letter

Using the second and third row of keys

47   there is a good supply of fruit out here

48   they helped us to get the apples pipped;

49   she said the pears were of good quality;

50   let the grass grow for the sheep to eat;

51   at their request those words were passed

52   please pass the pepper; we lost the salt

53   he requires a speedy reply to his query;

54   they are far too old to walk to the wood

55   wear the purple tie; pull the white rope

56   she was the first to walk past the post;

57   we will request a further supply of wool

58   look at the jewels; they are quite safe;

59   we are told there is quite a large queue

60   those last three pupils had good results

61   all the people greatly fear earthquakes;

62   perhaps they will stay at your old hotel

5 The first row of keys

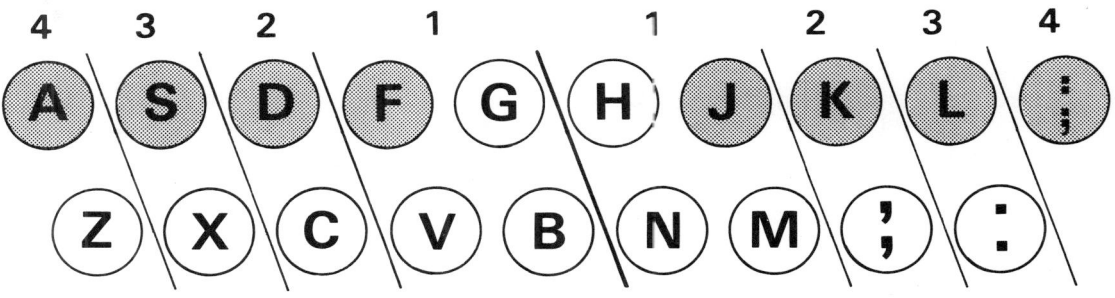

Fig. 13 The first row of keys

18

QUESTIONS
Write short answers to the following.
1 When typing dotted lines, how many spaces are left after the last word before the dots are started?
2 Name the part of the typewriter which is used to move the platen a small amount so that dotted lines are lowered slightly.
3 Why is it necessary to lower dotted lines slightly?

35 Circular letters
These are letters which are sent out by an organisation to a group of people. In each case the contents of the letter are identical, only the name and address of the recipient with perhaps an occasional detail, differing. A circular letter might be used, for example, when a school wishes to give information to parents; or when a business wishes to notify customers of price changes.

One popular method of producing circular letters is by ink duplicating. A master copy of the letter is typed on a stencil which is used in an ink duplicator to make the number of copies required.

An example of a circular letter is given in Fig. 33 (overleaf).

Note   (1)   The line spacing is similar to that for the business letter shown in Fig. 21 on page 67.
(2)   In the example above the name and address of the addressee is not required. If, however, this is to be inserted later, then adequate space (e.g. 8 single-line spaces) must be allowed between the reference and the salutation.
(3)   A space may be left in the salutation, e.g. Dear   so that names can be inserted later.
(4)   (a)   If the writer is to sign the master copy then the complimentary close is typed in the usual way.
(b)   If the writer is not signing, then his or her name can be typed.
(5)   When a letter has a tear-off portion at the end, it is separated from the letter by a line of continuous hyphens from edge to edge of the paper. Any blank spaces left for details to be entered are indicated by continuous full stops.

EXERCISES

Exercise 1
Copy the circular letter in single-line spacing in fully blocked style shown in Fig. 33. Use A4 paper (210 × 297 mm). Set margins at 12–72 (pica) or 22–82 (elite).

The fingers to be used for reaching from the guide keys to the first row are shown in Fig. 13. Only the operating finger should be moved downwards when a key in the first row is struck. The other fingers should retain their guide key position.

EXERCISES

It is recommended that each line should be typed at least three times.
Typing line: 40 spaces. Single-line spacing.

Keys N and B

1   jj nn jj nn jn jn nj nj jj njn jnnj njjn

2   ff bb ff bb fb fb bf bf ff bfb fbbf bffb

3   tin nap den no nine line ton din new nut

4   bay bat tab by bake bill bit boy bow bag

5   nob nib bone born none brand brown noble

6   been brain bring bank begin blind nibble

7   the boys took the blue boat into the bay

8   the angry dog nearly bit the naughty boy

9   both brothers went to buy nine new books

10   he is now able to bring the brown paint;

11   she has borrowed a beautiful blue blouse

12   listen to the band playing near the bank

Keys M and V

13   jj mm jj mm jm jm mj mj jj mjm jmmj mjjm

14   ff vv ff vv fv fv vf vf ff vfv fvvf vffv

15   my may met men map jam mat man whom lamp

16   van vat view vote give every vivid never

17   mad room from made home make mark motive

18   move live value over have visitor volume

Exercise 3

Display the following application form on a sheet of A5 paper. Take one carbon copy.

NETHERHALL SLIMMING CLUB

Visit to Padlow Grange Health Farm
(typist insert dates here)

Name of member _ _ _ _ _ _ _ _ _ _ _ _

Address _ _ _ _ _ _ _ _ _ _ _ _ _ _ _

_ _ _ _ _ _ _ _ _ _ _ _ _ _ _

_ _ _ _ _ _ _ _ _ _ _ _ _ _ _

Membership Nº _ _ _ _ _ _ _ _ _ _ _

Room required   * Double / single / with bath

————— * delete as required

I will / will not require transport

Using the top copy of the application

(a)   Insert details in respect of Mrs. Jean Moss of 4 Alderson Drive, Harrogate HG2 8AS whose membership number is H 7184. She would like a single room and will be travelling in her own car. Date and sign the form.

(b)   Type the envelope required to return the form to the Netherhall Slimming Club (for the attention of Miss R. Brook) Wheatley Hall Road, Rotherham RO7 6HT.

(Y.R.E.B.)

176

19 we may be moving to live with my mother;

20 many more visitors will be arriving soon

21 the new moon was shining over the valley

22 our van driver arrived late this morning

23 the five women were soon lost from view;

24 make them from the new vivid red velvet;

Keys C and ,

25 dd cc dd cc dc dc cd cd dd cdc dccd cddc

26 kk ,, kk ,, k, k, ,k ,k kk ,k, k,,k ,kk,

27 cup ace ice can cut cry cat cow cot come

28 cap, call, pace, came, mice, luck, deck,

29 cave crack knock comb creep cream career

30 car, back, lick, nice case, lock, clock;

31 collect a fancy cream cake frcm the shop

32 their child chose a crimson ccat and cap

33 she can cancel the order for cane chairs

34 children came to watch the circus clowns

35 call for, say, three cups, or maybe four

36 yes, she can come with you, but not yet;

Using keys NBMVC,

37 jnnj fbbf jmmj fvvf dccd k,,k nmb, vc,mn

38 they even had to remove some tins of mud

39 she took the cat and the browr dog home,

40 nobody meant to become lost ir the caves

Exercise 2

Type the form below on A4 paper, margins 10–72 (pica), 15–85 (elite), and then complete the form on behalf of Miss A Waterhouse, 19 Wentworth Road, Birmingham B17 7PH who wishes to go to the college on 25–27 August. Her first choice of course is Badminton, her second Fencing. She will require full board and residence. Date but do not sign the form.

```
              APPLICATION FORM FOR RESIDENTIAL COURSES

                    Newfields Residential College
                         Whitelands Road
                          Upton-on-Salt
                       Surrey    GU27 5PT


Name      ...................................................

Address   ...................................................

          ...................................................

          ...................................................

Dates of course  ...........................................

First choice of course  ....................................

Second choice of course  ...................................

I shall require full board and residence.        *YES/NO

I shall not require full residence but the following meals:

                              Friday  ...................

                              Saturday  .................

                              Sunday  ...................

*Delete as necessary.

A deposit of £5 must accompany each application.

Signed  .............................

Date  ...............................
```

41 the bomb can easily go off without care,

42 no, he cannot come, it is much too late,

43 my brother must never move that bookcase

44 new members may come back in the coaches

45 we can both remember to number the books

46 seven circus caravans are near the canal

47 command them to move their big black van

48 both cubs remained close to their mother

Keys X and .
Two spaces are left after a full stop at the end of a sentence.

49 ss xx ss xx sx sx xs xs ss xsx sxxs xssx

50 ll .. ll .. l. l. .l .l ll .l. l..l .ll.

51 six box mix tax extra export boxes exact

52 fix. exert. excite. anxious. excuse.

53 extra tax has to be paid on the exports.

54 they expect the six boxes to be returned

Key Z

55 aa zz aa zz az az za za aa zaz azza zaaz

56 zip zoo jazz prize zero size gaze dozen;

57 the crowds gazed at the blazing factory.

58 these five dozen zips are the wrong size

Using the letters of the alphabet

59 at the zoo we saw six zebras and a lion;

60 we are going to a pop concert in the car

34 Preparation and completion of forms

The filling in of forms is an essential part of everyday life.

Forms are usually printed with dotted lines for the answers.

When typing dotted lines, one space is left after the last word before the dots are started. The variable line spacer is used to move the platen a small amount so that dotted lines are lowered slightly. If this was not done, the typed answers would appear on top of the dots. After using the variable line spacer to produce dotted lines that are slightly down, the answers can be typed slightly above the dots.

EXERCISES

Exercise 1

Type the form below in double-line spacing on A5 portrait paper (148 × 210 mm) with margins set at 5–55 (pica), 12–62 (elite) and then fill in the details.

```
                   JOB APPLICATION FORM


Surname          ...........................................

First Names (in full)  .....................................

Address      ...............................................

Date of Birth      .........................................

School at present      .....................................

Date you can leave school  .................................

Examinations passed    .....................................

...........................................................

Examinations to be taken   .................................

...........................................................

Signature of Applicant     .................................

Date  .....................................................
```

Details for completion of form:
John Andrew Gray, 74 Stafford Street, Wolton   Date of Birth: 3.6.65
School: Wolton Secondary School   Date of leaving: July 1981
Examinations passed: R.S.A. Typewriting (Stage I), Commerce
Examinations to be taken: English Language, Maths, Science, French, History

61 at school there are four typing lessons.

6 The top row of keys

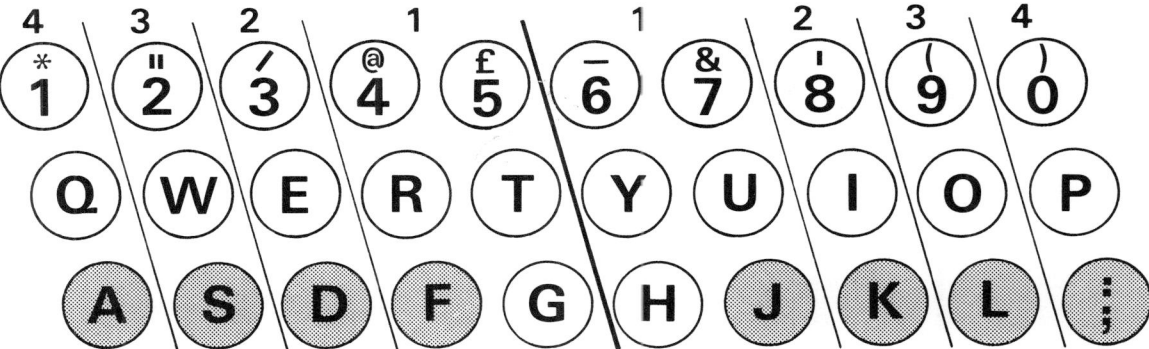

Fig. 14 The top row of keys

Figure 14 shows the fingers used for reaching from the guide keys to the top row. Each finger should go direct from the guide key to the figure key and back again.

This section introduces numbers and the hyphen. On some typewriters keys may not be provided for 1 and 0, and in these circumstances the figures may be obtained as follows: (**a**)   the letter 1 is used for figure 1,
(**b**)   the capital letter O is used for figure 0.

In order to type a capital letter O the left shift key (see Fig. 15) is depressed. Use of the shift keys is covered in the next chapter.

EXERCISES

It is recommended that each line should be typed at least three times.
Typing line: 40 spaces. Single-line spacing.

Keys 4 and 5

1   fr4 fr4 4rf 4rf f4 f4 4f 4f fr4 4rf 4fr4

2   fr5 fr5 5rf 5rf f5 f5 5f 5f fr5 ft5 gt5f

3   they bought 45 gallons of 4 star petrol;

4   there are 45 in class 5 on the 4th floor

Keys 7 and 6

5   ju7 ju7 7uj 7uj j7 j7 7j 7j ju7 7uj 7ju7

Exercise 2
Type the statement which appears below.

```
                        STATEMENT



              OFFICE SUPPLIERS AND CO LTD
                    14 Willow Way
                      TREEVILLE
                      TR7 3LE



B. Glum Ltd                              30 June 19--
30 Oak Street
TREEVILLE
TR7 3LE                                   Terms: Net
```

Date	Details	Debit	Credit	Balance
19--		£	£	£
June 1	Balance owing			857.19
June 3	Invoice No 31	20.90		878.09
June 7	Cheque		857.19	20.90
June 15	Invoice No 58	120.10		141.00
June 21	Invoice No 112	250.00		391.00
June 28	Credit Note No C12		91.00	300.00

Exercise 3
Type a statement from Sweet Supplies Ltd., of 34 Candy Road, Honeyville HO4 6LE to The Sugary Shop, 15 Cocoa Grove, Toffton TO9 6NO. Follow the layout given in Exercises 1 and 2 and insert the following details. Supply any additional details required.

Date: 31 December 19--.   Terms: net.

December 1	Balance owing	£749
December 5	Cheque	£749
December 10	Invoice No. 11	£150
December 15	Invoice No. 15	£200
December 18	Credit note No. C7	£25
December 21	Invoice No. 29	£350

Final balance: £675

6   ju6 ju6 6uj 6uj j6 j6 6j 6j ju6 jy6 hy6j

7   bring 7 pens, 46 pencils and 57 crayons;

8   77 boys and 64 girls; plus 55 tortoises.

Keys 3 and 8

9   de3 de3 3ed 3ed d3 d3 3d 3d de3 3ed 3de3

10   ki8 ki8 8ik 8ik k8 k8 8k 8k ki8 8ik 8ki8

11   38 boys and 38 girls make a total of 76;

12   played 85 games; won 76, drawn 3, lost 6

Using keys 345678

13   the number of the car key is 657, not 83

14   the telephone number of agent g5 is 874.

15   record number 3854 is listed on page 67.

16   my national insurance number is 654x378.

17   the number of his driving licence is c83

Keys 2 and 9

18   sw2 sw2 2ws 2ws s2 s2 2s 2s sw2 2ws 2sw2

19   lo9 lo9 9ol 9ol 19 19 91 91 lo9 9ol 9lo9

20   the team of 11 won 293 games out of 324;

21   22 pears, 39 apples, 92 plums, 8 grapes.

Keys 1 and 0

22   aql aql lqa lqa al al la la aql lqa laql

23   ;p0 ;p0 0p; 0p; ;0 ;0 0; 0; ;p0 0p; 0;p0

EXERCISES

Exercise 1

Type the statement of account which appears below.

STATEMENT

A SELLER LTD
4 Commerce Way
OLDTOWN
OL3 5WW

The Buyer Ltd   30 September 19--
The High Street
NEWTOWN
NE1 6WN   Terms: Net

Date	Details	Debit	Credit	Balance
19--		£	£	£
Sept 1	Balance owing			149.00
Sept 4	Cheque		149.00	
Sept 5	Invoice No 291	648.00		648.00
Sept 6	Invoice No 304	101.00		749.00
Sept 20	Credit Note No C81		27.60	721.00
Sept 27	Invoice No 906	104.00		825.40

24 there are 110 players in the tournament;

25 10 ships out of 11 were in the 1st class

Using numbers

26 4 new entries at 38, 27, 9 in the charts

27 36, 9, 5 and 4 are new entries this week

28 the serial number on the machine is z10;

29 10 times 10 is 100; 10 times 100 is 1000

30 quote the part number, that is, xf106930

31 14 women, 6 children and 35 men are here

32 buy 13 oranges, 14 pears and 15 peaches.

33 type question numbers 3, 5, 8, 9 and 14;

34 order 5 blue, 6 black and 7 red jumpers;

35 send goods numbered 23, 45, 68, 81, 1090

Key – (hyphen or dash)

A *hyphen* joins words together, e.g. mother-in-law. There is no space before or after a hyphen.

A *dash* is used for breaking up sentences, e.g. The hockey match – it was her first – was a complete success. There is a space both before and after a dash.

Using key –

36 ;p- ;p- -p; -p; ;- ;- -; -; ;p- -p; -;p-

37 mother-in-law has a self-contained flat;

38 he was a fair-haired, blue-eyed boy of 5

39 she may be tight-fisted and ill-tempered

40 do please take one - no, two - with you;

41 the answer is twelve - sorry - thirteen;

Exercise 3

On a suitable form type the following credit note from Office Suppliers & Co. Ltd., 64 Commercial Street, Newtown, NT1 41Z. Number C.84 dated 1 October 19––.

To: Churchfold Manufacturing Ltd.,
32 Industry Lane,
Wolverhampton WV4 5HH.

Reason for credit: damaged goods
Quantity and description: 1 'Robust' typewriter
Cost (excluding VAT): £161-50
VAT rate: 15%
VAT amount: £24-23
Total goods: £161-50
Total VAT: £24-23
Total amount credited: £185-73
Original invoice No. Z276 dated 6 September 19––

Statements of account

As mentioned at the beginning of this chapter, payment for most business transactions is not required immediately, and so the buyer is not expected to pay each invoice as it arrives. He waits to receive a statement of account listing all of the transactions which have taken place since the last statement was received. Thus usually at the end of each month, the supplier sends to the buyer a statement showing the following items: (1) any unpaid balance still owing to the seller at the beginning of that month from earlier months; (2) totals of invoices sent out during the month; (3) credits for any allowances; (4) amounts of cash received; (5) the unpaid balance.

The statement shows the terms of payment for the sum owing on the month's transactions. The purpose of this document is to request payment for the sum owing.

42   he is unable - due to illness - to come;

43   one-half - no, one-fifth - are failures;

7 The shift keys

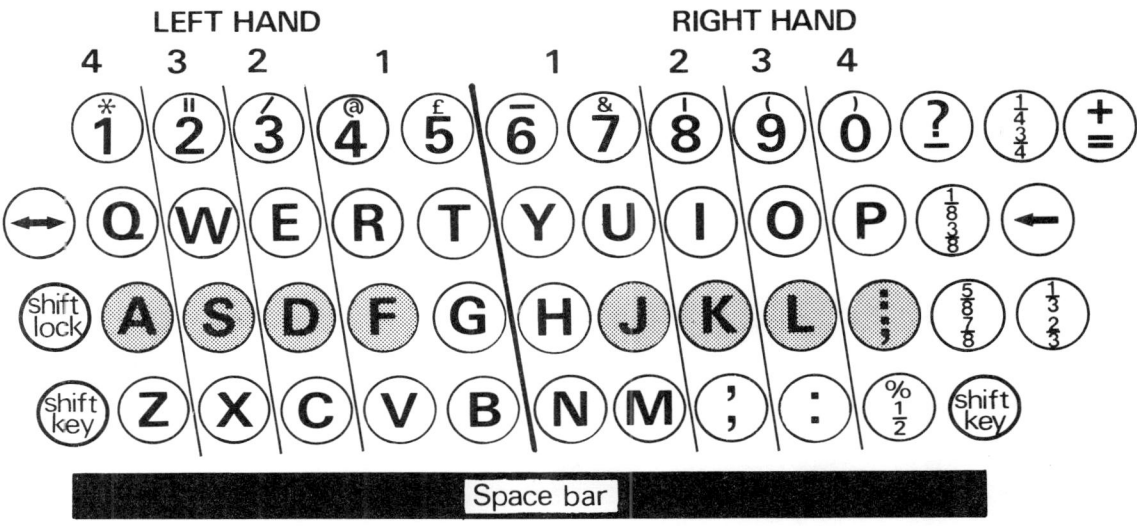

Fig. 15 The shift key and lock

There is a shift key on each side of the keyboard, usually at each end of the bottom row of keys (Fig. 15). This key is used for typing:

A capital letters,
B punctuation marks,
C miscellaneous characters.

All of these are known as *upper case* characters. *Lower case* is the term applied to those characters not requiring the use of the shift key. The shift keys are operated by the little fingers. After the shift key is released, the finger should return to its normal guide key position.

EXERCISES
It is recommended that each line should be typed at least three times.
    Typing line: 40 spaces. Single-line spacing.

Capital letters and colon

The *right shift key* is used to make capitals for letters typed by the left hand.

1   Aa Dd Ff Ss We Wear Fear Bat Sat Dart Go

Exercise 2

Type the credit note which appears below. In this example, VAT is not chargeable and so a simpler layout is used.

CREDIT NOTE

SCHOOL SUPPLIERS AND CO LTD
4 Trade Road
NEWTOWN
NT1 8IZ

Date: 1 July 19--

To: Head of English
    The Queen Elizabeth School
    BRIGHTVILLE
    BR7 8LE

Quantity	Description	Unit Price	Total Price
		£	£
10	Loose leaf books, returned damaged, 20 June, 19-- Invoice No P7604	0.35	3.50
1	Storage cover, 229 x 178, returned as above	0.25	0.25
	Total amount credited		£3.75

```
2  Top Arch Ruth Went Catch Every Goat Soar

3  Call on Sam, Reg, Wendy, Diane and Gail.

4  Tom and Dick will be in Dover on Sunday.

5  She will visit Aunt Edith next Saturday.
```

The *left shift key* is used to make capitals for letters typed by the right hand.

```
6  Ll Kk Jj John Mill Hop Kiln Upon Pink No

7  You: Know: Len: Moat Never Joke Point It

8  Please find Kate, Jack, Irene and Larry.

9  Joe York has sent the map to Peter Hill.

10 I saw Neil and Harry in Leeds on Monday.
```

Using right and left shift keys

```
11 At It Go No War; Queen: Heart Turf King:

12 There is a Disco Dance at the Glee Hall:

13 I must see Ron Rave, the new Disc Jockey

14 Kim Weston and I will leave in February.

15 Ask Paul Dale to see Mike and Roy Mills.
```

The *shift lock* is depressed when several capital letters are to be typed in succession. It is released by depressing a shift key.

```
16 ANN MARIE and RACHAEL were at the PARTY:

17 On MONDAY we take the late TRAIN to BATH

18 I read the DAILY GLOAT on the fast train

19 An END-OF-SEASON SALE at BLOGGS new shop

20 Visit LONDON, BIRMINGHAM and MANCHESTER.
```

Exercise 1

Type the credit note which appears below.

```
                            CREDIT NOTE


                            A SELLER LTD
                           4 Commerce Way
                          OLDTOWN OL3 5WW


    VAT Registration No 951 3246 21              Date: 20 September 19--


    B Buyer Ltd
    The High Street
    NEWTOWN
    NE1 6WN



    Invoice No M304
    Dated: 6 September 19--               Tax Point: 6 September 19--
```

Catalogue Number	Quantity	Description	Price Each	Cost	VAT Rate	VAT Amount
			£	£		£
3272	4 boxes	Crisps – returned damaged	6.00	24.00	15%	3.60
		Total Goods		24.00		
		Total VAT		3.60		
		Total amount credited		£27.60		

Punctuation marks

Spacing after punctuation marks

no space:
(1) Before or after a *hyphen*,
e.g. half-term; before or after an *apostrophe* when it comes before the s,
e.g. John's book.
(2) After an *opening bracket* or before a *closing bracket*,
e.g. that house (number four) is old.
(3) After an *opening quotation mark* or before a *closing quotation mark*,
e.g. "go home at once".

one space:
(1) After a *comma*, *colon* or *semicolon*.
(2) Before and after the hyphen used as a *dash*,
e.g. She will arrive soon - at least, I hope so.

two spaces:
After a *full stop*, an *exclamation mark* (see page 55) a *quotation mark* or a *question mark* at the end of a sentence.

EXERCISES

It is recommended that each line should be typed at least three times.
Typing line: 40 spaces. Single-line spacing.

Apostrophe and question mark

1   ki' ki' lk' jk' hk' 'uk 'pk d'k a'f 'kl'

2   ;p? ;p? lp? p?; fp? ?p; l?; ?j' 'k? ?;'k

3   Where is Joe's car? Why? I don't know:

4   What is the name of Helen's dog? Where?

Quotation marks

5   sw" sw" "ws "ws w"s ?s" "s' ps" "ws s"w"

6   "Will you collect my new shoes, please?"

7   "Can Sam's tennis racquet be re-strung?"

8   "Could you fetch my sister's new dress?"

Exercise 4

Type today's date on an invoice from School Suppliers and Co. Ltd., 4 Trade Road, Newtown NT1 81Z to The Art Department, Westfold School, Brightville BR7 8LE and fill in the following details:

2	Studio smocks @ £4.35	8-70
12	tins Coloured pencils @ 22p.	2-64
3	Lettering sets @ 75p.	2-25
2	pairs Asbestos gaunttets @ £3.	6-00
1	tin Powder paint, white @ £6.20	6-20
2	Gun tackers @ £6.	12-00
		£ 37-79

Terms: 2½% within 14 days

Credit Notes

A credit note is sent by the supplier to the buyer if it is necessary to reduce the amount charged on the invoice. This can happen in the following circumstances (1) when the buyer has been over-charged; (2) when the buyer returns damaged goods or goods sent by the supplier in error; (3) when packing cases, which have been charged to the buyer on the invoice, are returned.

Credit notes are usually printed and typed in red in order to distinguish them from other documents.

Bracket (or parenthesis)

9   lo(lo((ol (ol p(l w(l "l((4l 2(l (ll(

10 ;p) ;p))p;)p; u); t); ?;) ";) ';));;)

11 An out-of-season holiday (early in May):

12 Capitals (or upper case)? No, type 349:

Using punctuation marks

13 Do type question mark (?) and hyphen (-)

14 "Does this cost as much as those there?"

15 John's sister (MARY) is 12 years old now

16 "PLEASE pass me Tiny's new, red collar."

17 "Is it wet and windy?" "No, dry" I said

Miscellaneous characters

EXERCISES
It is recommended that each line should be typed at least three times.
  Typing line: 40 spaces. Single-line spacing.

£ and __ (underscore)
The underscore key is used for underlining.
Note   When underlining is necessary follow this procedure:
   (1)   the letters or words must first be typed;
   (2)   the carriage is returned until the typing point appears under the first letter
         to be underlined (Fig. 16);

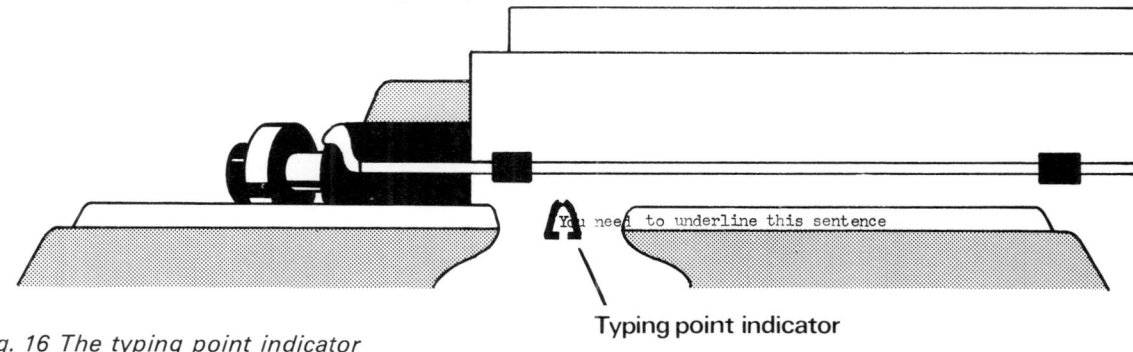

Fig. 16 The typing point indicator

Typing point indicator

Exercise 3

Type the invoice which appears below. In this example VAT is not chargeable and so a simpler layout is used.

```
                                                  No P7604

                         INVOICE


             SCHOOL SUPPLIERS AND CO LTD
                    4 Trade Road
                    NEWTOWN
                    NT1 8IZ

                                      Date: 11 June 19--

   To: Head of English
       The Queen Elizabeth School
       BRIGHTVILLE
       BR7 8LE
```

Quantity	Description	Unit Price	Total Price
		£	£
36	Storage cover, 229 x 178	0.25	9.00
10	Clasp files	0.75	7.50
12	Box files, spring clip, A4	0.70	8.40
12 doz	Biro pens, clear plastic	0.60	7.20
60	Wooden rulers, 30 cm	0.90	4.50
60	Loose leaf books	0.35	21.00
	Total		£57.60
	Terms: 2½% within 14 days		

    (3)   the back space key or carriage release lever is used in returning the carriage (use of the carriage return lever would turn up the paper);

    (4)   the shift lock may be used if several letters are to be underscored.

1   `ju_ ju_ jy_ jy_ _uj _uj y_j y_j j6_ iju_`

2   `fr£ fr£ ft£ ft£ £rf £rf t£f t£f t5£ "fr£`

3   `jug fat cup gloat £97 (£100); I "Bill's"`

4   `Do they read the TELEGRAPH or the TIMES?`

5   `No order accepted before the 1st of May:`

& (ampersand) and @ (at)

6   `ju& ju& ku& u&j &uj 1&2 2&3 6&7 7&8 45&9`

7   `fr@ fr@ @rf @rf r@f r@f 3 @ 38 4 @ 73 @f`

8   `Smith & Brown: 12 & 13 HIGH STREET; &@&@`

9   `Order 9 @ £5; 16 @ £24; 37 @ £4; 2 @ £8.`

10   `White & Green ordered 50 @ £5 and 4 @ £6`

/ (oblique) and % (percentage)

11   `de/ de/ /ed /ed e/d e/d 6/7 5/6 a/b/m/c/`

12   `;% ;% %; %; 1%; 3%; 5%; 7%; 9%; 10%; 2%;`

13   `I do/don't require lunch/tea/dinner now:`

14   `Is the number of your licence AB/90/X/V?`

15   `Smith & Company have 75% of the markets.`

Fractions

In addition to the $\frac{1}{2}$ key most typewriters have keys with other fractions (Fig. 9). These are typed with the little (;) finger.

    Some will require the use of the shift key.

    As soon as a fraction has been typed, the finger should return to its normal guide key position.

16   `;½ ;½ ½; ½; 1½; 3½; 9½; 10½; 6½; 7½%; ;½`

17   `;p¾ ;p¾ ¾p; ;p¼ ;p¼ ¼p; ¼p; 1¾; 3¼; 24¾;`

Exercise 2

Type the invoice which appears below. Insert the paper in the typewriter and set margin tab stops at the appropriate points for each column.

```
                                                        No 1654

                          INVOICE


                       A SELLER LTD
                      4 Commerce Way
                         OLDTOWN
                         OL3 5WW


VAT Registration No 951 3246 21              Date: 6 September 19--


B Buyer Ltd
The High Street
NEWTOWN
NE1 6WN


Your Order No 246                      Tax Point: 6 September 19--
```

Catalogue Number	Quantity	Description	Price Each	Cost	VAT Rate	VAT Amount
			£	£		£
3241	50	Crisps	8.00	400.00	15%	60.00
3263	50	Crisps	8.00	400.00	15%	60.00
3272	100	Crisps	6.00	600.00	15%	90.00
		Total Goods		1 400.00		£210.00
		Total VAT		210.00		
		Total amount due		£1 610.00		
E & O E						

18 Sales are 12½% up; purchases are 9¾% up:

19 9¼ @ £7; 16½ @ £23; 4¾ @ £4; 19½ @ £100:

Using miscellaneous characters

20 Order 200 @ £40 less 15½% before May 31:

21 JONES & SIMPSON'S profit has jumped 19%.

22 Do you buy fish/chips/peas/bread weekly?

23 24¼% of those asked bought chips weekly.

Using the shift keys

24 "Send by return of post FIVE (5) @ £28."

25 "Is the number of Joe's typewriter X/4?"

26 The TUCK SHOP opens for ten (10) minutes

27 My address is 19 High Road, NEWTOWN SE8.

28 Three-quarters (¾) of us have BLUE eyes:

QUESTIONS

Write short answers to the following.

1 State briefly the importance of the guide keys.
2 Write down the guide keys for (a) the left hand, (b) the right hand.
3 The space bar is always struck with the _____.
4 If a key is not provided for the number one, the letter _____ is used.
5 If a key is not provided for the figure nought, the capital letter _____ is used.
6 A _____ is a punctuation mark which is used to join two or more words together.
7 A _____ is a punctuation mark which is used for breaking up sentences.
8 State the spacing required before or after (a) a hyphen, (b) a dash.
9 Give three uses of the shift keys.
10 State the meaning of the term *lower case*.
11 The right shift key is used to make capitals typed by the _____ hand.
12 When several capital letters are to be typed, the _____ is depressed.
13 How many spaces are left after a comma, colon or semicolon?
14 How many spaces are left after a full stop, an exclamation mark, a quotation mark or a question mark at the end of a sentence?
15 The _____ key is used for underlining.

Invoices

The invoice or bill sent by the seller to the buyer provides a summary of a transaction. The purpose of the document is to notify the buyer of the amount due.

Note   (1)   An invoice often has the abbreviation E. and O.E. (Errors and Omissions Excepted) printed on it, meaning that the invoice is correct apart from any errors or omissions. The purpose is to safeguard the supplier against loss from such mistakes. For example, if a mistake has been made in calculating the amount owing on the invoice, the supplier reserves the right to correct the mistake.

(2)   Value added tax (VAT) is a tax payable on any goods and services which fall within its scope. Traders registered with HM Customs and Excise for VAT purposes are obliged to provide information on invoices showing rates, amounts and registration numbers. Tax point is the date when VAT is officially chargeable. This is usually the date when goods are delivered or invoiced.

(3)   The 'terms' refers to the terms of payment. If payment is made to the seller within 14 days, a cash discount of $2\frac{1}{2}\%$ may be deducted by the buyer from the amount due. The purpose of cash discount is to encourage prompt payment.

EXERCISES

Exercise 1

Type today's date on an invoice from Visual Manufacturers Ltd., 3 Clear Street, Mantown MA1 6WN to Midland Photographic Supplies Ltd., 57 Chiswick Street, Wolton WO4 7TO and fill in the following details:

Goods supplied	£	£
1 Leica M3	150·00	150-00
1 Cannon SD	49·50	49·50
6 Aluminium cases	19·50	117-00
3 Projection screens	10·90	32-70
2 F. 30 enlargers	28·00	56-00
		405-20
Less 10% Trade Discount		40·52
		364-68

Terms:
2½% within 14 days

Note   Trade discount is a deduction made by the supplier from catalogue prices. The discount represents the buyer's gross profit margin.

III PRACTISING THE KEYBOARD

8 Measurements, money and time

Numbers
When typing numbers a space is used to separate millions from thousands and thousands from hundreds.

For example: 2 345 000   42 240   101 201

Note   A space between thousands and hundreds is *not* used when typing years, e.g. (a) 1802, 1981; or (b) if there are only four numbers in the text, e.g. There are 1200 pupils in school.

EXERCISES
It is recommended that each line should be typed at least three times.

Typing line: 60 spaces. Single-line spacing.

1   There are spaces for 5000 cars or 10 500 motor cycles.

2   A population of 23 742 000 males and 22 651 000 females.

3   In 1973 there were 121 732 accidents reported.

4   A crowd of 55 742 watched the game last week.

5   There were 250 000 in the armed forces in 1978.

Measurements
1   Generally, one space is left between the number and unit of measurement, e.g. 8 metres, 12 centimetres.

2   A full stop is not required after abbreviations of measurements, unless at the end of a sentence. For example

1 kg (1 kilogram),   43 cm (43 centimetres),

10 m (10 metres),   210 mm (210 millimetres),

5 ft 6 in (5 feet 6 inches),   4 lb 3 oz (4 pounds 3 ounces).

Note   Abbreviations do not take an s in the plural.
For example 3 yd (3 yards), 20 km (20 kilometres).
There are **two exceptions**: litre(s) and tonne(s) are typed in full to avoid any confusion. For example 1 litre, 2 litres, 1 tonne, 10 tonnes.

Exercise 2

Prepare an order form on A4 paper as described in Exercise 1. Complete the order form by ordering the following plants from Timms & Timms Ltd., Garden Suppliers, Brailes, Oxon. OX15 7BL for Mr. D. Spendlove, 93 Foregate Street, Worcester WO17 4QZ.

> 3 Bush roses named Red Devil
> 3 Climbing roses – Whiskey Mac, Super Star, Firecrest
> 3 Miniature roses – Pour Toi
> 2 Shrubs – Leylandii

The roses are all priced at 45p each and the shrubs are 35p each. Use today's date. The order number is 347. Delivery instructions are 'prompt delivery, carriage paid'.

(LREB – adapted)

Exercise 3

Type the order which appears below. Place a sheet of A5 paper over the exercise and trace the lines with a pencil and ruler. Insert the paper in the typewriter and set margin and tab stops at the appropriate points for each column.

PRAXITELES PRODUCTIONS LIMITED

ORDER FORM

Date:

Catalogue Reference Number	Title	Media and Format	Price
F6138	Business Organisations	Film Strip	£ 3.25
F4139	Trading Account	Film Strip	3.25
F5140	Commercial Documents	Film Strip	3.25
L7026	Profit & Loss Account	Film Loop	2.85
L7031	Sources of Capital	Film Loop	2.85
C2092	Accounting machines	Wallchart	0.40
C2103	Stencil Duplicating	Wallcharts	1.05
AVP382	Careers in Business	Audio-Visual Pack	6.10
SF3724	Building Societies	Study Folder	0.95
SF3813	The Stock Exchange	Study Folder	1.10
SF3507	Hire Purchase	Study Folder	0.75
SF3762	British Insurance	Study Folder	0.75

FROM:	Tutor in Charge Commerce Department College of Further Education West Park LEEDS LS6 2JA	TOTAL	~~26.55~~ 20.70
		VAT	~~2.12~~ 1.66
		SMALL ORDER CHARGE	
		TOTAL AMOUNT ENCLOSED	~~28.67~~ 22.36

(R.S.A.)

3 The letter x can be used in place of the word *by* in measurements. One space is left before and after the x. For example 7 m x 3 m, 200 mm x 194 mm.

4 Groups of figures and measurements should not be divided at the end of lines.

EXERCISES
It is recommended that each line should be typed at least three times.
  Typing line: 50 spaces. Single-line spacing.

1 A4 typing paper measures 210 mm x 297 mm.

2 A5 portrait paper is 148 mm x 210 mm.

3 A5 landscape paper measures 210 mm x 148 mm.

4 The rug measured 1 m x 2 m.

5 Buy 6 lb of parsnips and 2 lb of peas.

6 Jean is 5 ft 3 in in height.

7 Put 6 litres in to the tank, please.

8 The prize marrow weighed 5 lb 7 oz.

Decimals
The full stop is used to type a decimal point and there is no space before or after. For example 34.65, 8.25.

EXERCISES
It is recommended that each line should be typed at least three times.
  Typing line: 50 spaces. Single-line spacing.

1 Write down 9.30, 7.45, 18.05, 22.60 and 0.81.

2 The area measures 4.310 x 1.500 m.

3 One box weighs 41.703 kg; the other is 23.201 kg.

4 You buy 7.5 litres today and 9.5 litres tomorrow.

5 The town is 20.25 km from this city.

Sums of money
1 *Pounds only* Any sum can be typed with or without the decimal point. For example £3, £25, £6 770 (or £3.00, £25.00, £6 770.00).
Note   No space is left after the £ sign.

```
                                        Order No   246


                        B  BUYER  LTD
                      The  High  Street
                        NEWTOWN
                        NE1  6WN


      A Seller Ltd
      4 Commerce Way
      OLDTOWN
      OL3 5WN                       Date:   1 September 19--


      Please supply:
```

Quantity	Goods	Cost
50 Boxes	Ready salted crisps	£8.00 per box
50 Boxes	Oxo flavoured crisps	£8.00 per box
100 Boxes	Curry flavoured crisps	£6.00 per box
	Delivery instructions: (prompt delivery), carriage paid	
	SIGNED	

```
                                    for  B  Buyer  Ltd
```

2 *Pence only* Amounts less that £1 can be typed with or without the £ symbol and decimal point. For example 10p, 45p; (or £0.10, £0.45).

The halfpenny is typed as a fraction. For example 34½p, (or £0.34½).

When the £ symbol is not used, the pence can be shown either with the word pence typed in full or with the abbreviation p, for example 10 pence or 10p.

A full stop is not used after the abbreviation p except at the end of sentence.

Note No space is left between figures and the abbreviation p.

3 *Mixed amounts of pounds and pence* The decimal point and £ sign are used. For example £18.10, £453.75. Two figures always appear after the decimal point in order to avoid confusion between sums like £11.05—(5p) and £11.50—(50p).

The £ symbol and the pence abbreviation should not be included together in a single money expression. For example £12.25 and **not** £12.25p.

Note A sum of money represented as figures should not be divided at the end of a line of typing.

EXERCISES

It is recommended that each line should be typed at least three times.

Typing line: 60 spaces. Single-line spacing.

1   The items cost £5, £36, £110 and £4 397 respectively.

2   The book is 75p, the fruit is 48½p; a total of £1.23½.

3   Prepare tickets for £9.45, £24.60, £38.15 and £229.50.

4   The fare is £24.10 for an adult and £12.05 for a child.

5   A ticket machine takes 5p, 10p and 50p coins - not 2p coins.

Time

A full stop is not required after abbreviations of time unless at the end of a sentence.

For example 9 15 am (ante meridiem), 12 30 pm (post meridiem).

Note One space is left between the figures and the letters. One space is left between the hours and minutes.

EXERCISES

It is recommended that each line should be typed at least three times.

Typing line: 60 spaces. Single-line spacing.

1   The office opens at 8 45 am and closes at 5 30 pm.

2   There are separate shows at 2 pm, 5 pm, and 8 pm.

3   Parking is prohibited between 3 30 am and 6 15 pm.

VII DOCUMENTS

33 Commercial transactions

In the business world, the buying and selling of goods and services is done usually on credit, that is, goods are dispatched by the supplier in advance of payment by the buyer. Each transaction is recorded by a series of documents showing value received by the buyer and the amount owing to the supplier.

Documents vary in style and layout but the general principles involved in their use are the same.

Orders

The purpose of an order sent to a seller is to provide a statement of the quantity and type of goods required by the buyer. It may take the form of a letter, but usually it is on a printed order form.

EXERCISES

Exercise 1

Type the order which appears overleaf. Insert the paper in the typewriter and set margin and tab stops at the appropriate points for each column.

This exercise is in fully blocked style. Begin the first character in the column beneath the first letter of the heading.

The 24-hour clock

The 24-hour clock is often used to indicate time. Some examples of 24-hour clock times are as follows:

12 30 am	0030
4 30 am	0430
9 00 am	0900
noon	1200
2 10 pm	1410
6 00 pm	1800
9 00 pm	2100
midnight	0000

EXERCISES

It is recommended that each line should be typed at least three times:
   Typing line: 60 spaces. Single-line spacing.

1   The match begins at 1500 hours and ends at 1640 hours.

2   Trains run at 0015 hours, 0630 hours, and 1020 hours.

3   The show is televised between 2015 hours and 2145 hours.

4   The meeting begins at 1400 hours and ends at 1630 hours.

5   Flights for London leave at 0900 hours and 1200 hours.

QUESTIONS

Write short answers to the following.
1   When typing numbers, millions are separated from thousands and thousands from hundreds by a _____ .
2   Generally, abbreviations of measurements do not take an s in the plural. Two exceptions which are typed in full are 1 _____ and t _____ .
3   Which letter can be used in place of *by* in measurements?
4   A decimal point is typed by using the _____ .
5   In typing sums of money, how does the halfpenny appear?
6   The abbreviation for *pence* is _____ .
7   Which of the following is typed correctly?
   (a) £15.75   (b) £0.45p   (c) £10.05
8   Give the 24-hour clock times for the following.

5 30 am	4 30 pm
9 00 am	7 15 pm
noon	10 45 pm

Exercise 3
Type the following table.

TRADE STATISTICS

(Turn up 2 single lines) Foreign Imports	Years ended 30 June (Turn up 1 single line)		
	(Turn up 2 single lines) 1980 (Turn up 1 single line)	1981	1982
	Tonnes	Tonnes	Tonnes
Flour and grain	1 574 000	1 596 400	1 674 300
Animal feeding stuffs	500 300	380 700	341 700
Meat - fresh	85 300	88 400	77 900
Meat - preserved	37 400	38 600	39 200
Tea	43 700	44 200	41 300
Other food	19 100	21 800	22 900

QUESTIONS
Write short answers to the following.
1 What is the meaning of tabulation?
2 When typing sums of money in blocked style, the £ sign is blocked at the start of the _____ est line.
3 In order to type double lines underneath totals of figures, the platen must be freed by use of the _____.
4 In a _____ table, the column headings are separated from the column items by horizontal lines.
5 In a _____ table, there are vertical lines as well as horizontal lines.
6 The sides of a boxed table may be either _____ or closed in by vertical lines.
7 When there are varying widths of line in a column it is advisable to insert _____ to help guide the eye from one column to another.

9 Sentences

EXERCISES

It is recommended that each line should be typed at least three times.
  Typing line: 40 spaces. Single-line spacing.

1 Do please clean your machines every day.

2 A wise person has a careful tongue.

3 John is a wizard with a football.

4 If a lesson is missed, it means that
   extra work will have to be done.

5 She paid a deposit of £50; repayments
   will be 95p weekly.

6 Yesterday I bought an old car which is
   called 'Susie'. The seller offered a
   10% reduction for payment in cash.

7 I think that I shall re-name the car as
   either Liz or Alice. Which name would
   you choose?

Typing line: 60 spaces. Double-line spacing.

8 Every shopper knows that there are several kinds of shop.

   The main differences lie in what the shops sell and in their

   size.

9 Some shops sell clothes; others sell groceries and a whole

   host of other things.

10 The main kinds of shops are: (1) small shops; (2) department

    stores; (3) chain stores; (4) co-operative retail society

    shops; (5) self-service shops; (6) supermarkets; and also

    (7) hypermarkets.

Exercise 2
Type the following statement.

MUSIC RECORD COMPANY LTD

Section of Balance Sheet as at 30 September 1982

	1982	1981
	£	£
Subsidiary Companies		
Shareholdings	27 086 612	26 923 251
Indebtedness	12 960 843	10 083 356
	30 739 125	28 866 037
Current Assets		
Quoted Investments	1 637 691	1 379 335
Stocks	272 876	280 925
Debtors	2 634 247	2 883 099
Taxation recoverable	2 046 618	2 934 435
Treasury Bills	-	148 630
Deposits with local authorities	2 115 446	1 314
Cash and bank balances	1 519 475	1 267 394
	£10 226 353	£8 895 132

Typing line: 50 spaces. Single-line spacing.

11 Some producers prefer to sell direct to customers
in their homes rather than through shops. Many
types of products are sold direct, including some
<u>plastic household containers</u>, <u>cosmetic</u> and <u>skin
care preparations</u>, and <u>lingerie</u>.

12 Mail order firms operate through part-time agents.
The latter are employed to obtain <u>orders</u> and to
collect <u>payments</u> from customers.

Typing line: 60 spaces. Double-line spacing.

13 The sale of goods by SLOT MACHINES offers buyers the
chance of buying for 24 hours each day for 7 days a week.

14 If an article is bought for £1 and sold for £1.50 then the
gross profit is 50p (or 50% on the purchase price).

15 A bank has 3 functions: (1) to accept deposits, (2) to act
as an agent for payment, and (3) to lend money.

16 Money can be deposited in either a <u>current</u> account or a
<u>deposit</u> account, or in both. Another type of account is
called a <u>savings</u> account.

Typing line: 50 spaces. Double-line spacing.

17 When goods are bought on hire purchase, a deposit
has to be paid, and the remainder of the purchase
price plus the hire purchase charges are payable
over a fixed period.

18 The cash price of a motor cycle is £312. If the
machine is bought on hire purchase, the customer
pays a deposit of £105 and then £3.30 a week over
18 months.

32 Leader dots

When there are varying widths of line in a column it is advisable to insert leader dots to help guide the eye from one column to another.

Leader dots are made by using the full stop to type continuous dots .... Care should be taken to ensure that

(a) there is at least one space between the end of a word and the start of the dots :

(b) the dots do not run into the word they connect :

(c) the typing line does not extend beyond the last leader dot.

EXERCISES

Exercise 1
Type on A5 paper.

```
Carriage and Packing Charges

Retail orders for all Nursery Stock and/or
Garden Furniture exceeding £50 - carriage and
packing charges are free if payment is made
at the time of ordering.

This concession applies to customers in England,
Scotland and Wales only and does not include
the Channel Islands, Northern Ireland and over-
seas.

On prepaid orders below £50, carriage and
packing charges are as follows:

Order value up to £3.00 ............ add £0.85
Over £3.00 to £6.00 ............... add £1.50
Over £6.00 to £12.00 .............. add £2.50
Over £12.00 to £20.00 ............. add £3.75
Over £20.00 to £35.00 ............. add £5.00
Over £35.00 to £50.00 ............. add £6.00

YOU CAN SAVE THESE EXPENSES by collecting your
order from our Cash and Carry Centre. For Nursery
Stock please give us 48 hours' notice of your
visit.

OPEN

Monday to Friday          0900-1700
Saturday                  1000-1400
Sunday                    1100-1500
Easter and Bank Holidays  1000-1600
```

10 Paragraphs

Indented	Blocked	Hanging

(handwritten note: techincally no space.)

Fig. 17 Paragraphs

Paragraphs help the reader by breaking up writing into short passages. Three different styles of paragraphs are shown in Fig. 17.

Blocked Paragraphs

Note   There is (1) double-line spacing between blocked paragraphs typed in single-line spacing;
(2) treble-line spacing between blocked paragraphs typed in double-line spacing.

EXERCISES

Exercise 1

Typing line: 50 spaces. Single-line spacing.

```
A person with a bank account may be able to borrow
from the bank.  Borrowing may take the form of
either a loan or an overdraft.

If the bank manager grants an overdraft of £2 000,
this means that cheques can be written until the
customer owes the bank £2 000.

With an ordinary loan, the customer borrows all
the loan at once and repays in agreed instalments
with interest.
```

Exercise 2

Typing line: 60 spaces. Double-line spacing.

```
Two years ago a friend of mine decided to spend his holiday

camping by the side of a lake high in the mountains.  It was

a very remote place, miles away from any village and the

only way to reach it was on foot or on horseback.
```

Exercise 2
Type the following and rule. Use blocked style.

CAR ALLOWANCES

TOWN	PENCE PER MILE		
	CARLISLE	NEWCASTLE	BLACKPOOL
Barrow	22.5p	21.2p	23.2p
Darlington	22.5p	23.5p	21.5p
Kendal	23.0p	23.2p	23.0p
Morecambe	23.2p	23.2p	23.5p
Middlesborough	23.5p	24.2p	21.0p
Appleby	20.5p	23.5p	21.2p

Exercise 3
Display the following table and rule. Use blocked style.

BANK LOANS

Amount Borrowed	Monthly Repayment			
	3 years	5 years	7 years	10 years
£ 200	£ 7.56	£ 5.08	£ 4.38	£ 3.10
500	18.89	12.70	10.51	9.01
750	28.33	19.04	15.76	13.51
1000	37.38	25.39	21.02	18.02

Many of his friends told him that they thought he was very

unwise to camp in such a place as no one had been there for

many years.

It took him two days to reach his destination and as he

approached the lake he was extremely surprised to see a tiny

hut half hidden by trees.

Indented Paragraphs
In this form of paragraph the first line starts five spaces from the margin. The quickest way of starting new indented paragraphs is to use the tabulator which moves the carriage to any predetermined position. Figure 18 shows the three tabulator controls.

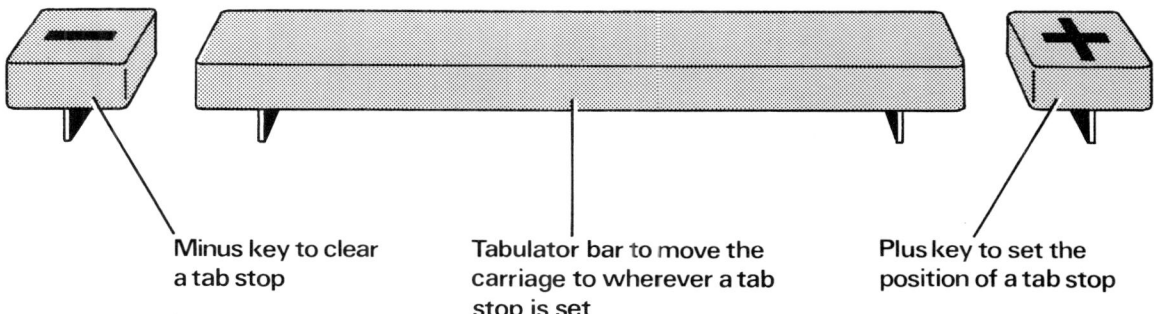

Minus key to clear   Tabulator bar to move the   Plus key to set the
a tab stop   carriage to wherever a tab   position of a tab stop
                          stop is set

Fig. 18 The tabulator

To set a tabulator stop, the space bar is tapped five times from the left-hand margin and a stop set at this point (i.e. 1.25 cm or half an inch).
Note   There is double-line spacing between indented paragraphs typed in *either* single- or double-line spacing.

EXERCISES

Exercise 1
Typing line: 60 spaces. Single-line spacing. Set tab stop for indenting 1.25 cm (half an inch).

        In the 18th century, a shopkeeper usually lived over
his shop with his family. Shops were small and a shopkeeper
employed at most 1 or 2 assistants. Employees 'lived in'.

        Hours of work were long. The shop opened at 8 am and
remained open until 10 pm (midnight on Saturdays).

Exercise 1
Type the following and rule. Use blocked style.

OVERNIGHT ALLOWANCES

CITY	BED AND BREAKFAST		
	FRIDAY	SATURDAY	SUNDAY
	£	£	£
London	12.50	13.50	12.00
Birmingham	11.25	12.25	11.75
Newcastle	10.75	11.25	11.00
Manchester	11.50	12.50	12.00
Edinburgh	12.00	13.00	11.50
Cardiff	11.50	12.50	12.00
Plymouth	10.50	11.00	10.75

Exercises 2 and 3

Typing line: 60 spaces. Double-line spacing. Set tab stop for indenting 1.25 cm (half an inch).

A hundred years ago everything was delivered to the shop in bulk. Sugar, rice and flour were kept in <u>sacks</u>; butter and currants were stored in <u>barrels</u>; tea was kept in <u>chests</u>; and cheeses were wrapped in <u>muslin</u>.

Orders had to be weighed and packed for each customer.

Exercise 3

A 19th century grocer stocked the following items; tea, coffee, cocoa, chicory, chocolate, spices, bird seed, flour, semolina, sauces, pepper and barley.

Although similar goods can be bought in a modern grocer's shop, their appearance is quite different. Do you think that today's grocery products are more hygienic?

Hanging Paragraphs

In this form of paragraph the first line starts 2 spaces to the left of the following lines. Thus the first line begins at the margin and 2 spaces are indented for all subsequent lines.

Note   There is double-line spacing between hanging paragraphs typed in *either* single- *or* double-line spacing.

EXERCISES

Exercise 1

Typing line: 50 spaces. Single-line spacing. Set tab stop for indenting 2 spaces.

Standards exist for many products. They are used
  as guides for quality, health and safety. Food
  standards are checked by Public Health people.

Cleanliness in food shops is vitally important.
  If regulations governing food cleanliness are
  not observed, there is a danger that consumers
  will suffer food-poisoning.

31 Sub-divided column headings

Some tabulations have columns with sub-divisions. Each sub-division may have a main heading and there may be separate headings for each sub-division.

In *blocked style*, the starting point for sub-divided headings will be the left-hand margin and the tab stops set for each column.

All column headings are placed on the same horizontal line which will be the starting point for the deepest heading.

Figures in columns must have units under units and tens under tens, etc. The £ sign is blocked above the first figure in the longest line.

Example

The table below is to be typed on A5 portrait paper (148 × 210 mm) in double-line spacing. Centre the whole table vertically and horizontally on the paper. Use blocked style. Leave three spaces between columns.

<u>BALANCE OF PAYMENTS (£m)</u>

(Turn up 3 single lines)

Year	Visible Account *(Turn up 2 single lines)* *(Turn up 1 single line)*		Balance
	Imports *(Turn up 2 single lines)*	Exports *(Turn up 1 single line)*	
	£ *(Turn up 2 single lines)*	£ *(Turn up 2 single lines)*	£
1978	12 115	14 468	2 353
1979	16 538 *(Turn up 2 single lines)*	21 732	5 194
1980	19 461	22 664	3 203
1981	25 416	28 987	3 571

(Turn up 1 single line)

Exercise 2
Typing line: 50 spaces. Double-line spacing. Set tab stop for indenting 2 spaces.

```
National morning newspapers are used by those

    advertisers who want their advertisements to be

    seen by as many people as possible.
Local papers serve a particular town or district

    and are used by advertisers who sell in the

    area.
```

Division of words at line-endings
Every attempt has to be made to avoid an uneven right-hand margin. It is sometimes necessary, therefore, to break words and carry over a part to the next line.

Warning of the approach of the end line of typing is given by the *bell* when only 5 or 6 spaces are left before the carriage locks at the margin. At that moment it becomes necessary to decide whether the word can be finished on the line or not.

Words are divided by the hyphen which is placed at the *end* of the line only. For example:

```
    Make sure you do not give unnecessary infor-

mation when completing an application form.
```

The best guide for dividing words is common-sense. More formal rules are listed in Appendix I.

Sometimes a word cannot easily be divided and must be completed, therefore, by extending the right-hand margin. The *margin release* key is used to type past the set margin.

EXERCISES
Read the rules for division of words (Appendix I) and then type each exercise three times. Note where the word is divided and where division is not possible.

Exercise 1
Typing line: 50 spaces. Double-line spacing.

```
micro-scope, con-tain, let-ter, neces-sary,

un-able, dis-appoint, harm-less, help-ful,

William, piece,
```

Exercise 4

Use a sheet of A4 paper. Display the following. Arrange the items into numerical order according to Plot Numbers starting with the lowest number.

QUEENSWAY HOMES LIMITED

'YEW TREE HILLS'

KNOWLE

Price List

Effective January 1980

Plot No	House Type	Kind	Freehold/ Leasehold	Price £
153	Oxford	Semi-detached	Freehold	16 000
194	Warwick GF	Maisonette	Leasehold	14 000
45	Dakota	Detached	Freehold	25 000
191	Warwick FF	Maisonette	Leasehold	13 000
150	Oxford	Semi-detached	Freehold	15 000
46	Dakota	Detached	Freehold	23 500
193	Warwick FF	Maisonette	Leasehold	13 000
151	Oxford	Semi-detached	Freehold	15 250
155	Oxford	Semi-detached	Freehold	15 000
192	Warwick GF	Maisonette	Leasehold	14 000

Ground rent for Maisonettes - £26.00 per annum

All types have warm air central heating and a garage

Typist! Underscore the headings as indicated.

(W.M.E.B.)

Exercise 2

Read through Appendix I again and then type the following using a hyphen to show a suitable line-end division. Underline any word which should not be divided.

Typing line: 50 spaces. Double-line spacing.

```
Pica, 10 000, murmur, problem, Friday, case,

success, obey, Sandra, London, excellent,

there, interrupted,
```

Exercise 3

Type the following using a hyphen to indicate the point where a suitable division might be made at the end of a line. Underline where a division should not be made.

Typing line: 50 spaces. Double-line spacing.

```
£1 042, spending, displeased, 1979, dictation,

rubber, Australia, U.S.A., transact, height,

please, through,
```

QUESTIONS

Write short answers to the following.

1 Name three different styles of paragraph.
2 There is _____ line spacing between blocked paragraphs typed in single-line spacing.
3 There is treble-line spacing between blocked paragraphs typed in _____ line spacing.
4 Name the type of paragraph which begins five spaces from the margin.
5 Which key is used to start an indented paragraph quickly?
6 There is _____ line spacing between indented paragraphs.
7 Name the type of paragraph in which the first line starts two spaces to the left of the following lines.
8 There is _____ line spacing between hanging paragraphs.
9 A warning of the approach of the end of the line of typing is given by the _____.
10 Words are divided at the end of a line by the use of a _____.
11 When necessary, a set margin can be extended by the use of the _____ key.

Exercise 3

Type a copy of the following table on A4 paper, taking care with the ruling. Use fully blocked style.

MEADOWLAND BRANCH SALES
1974 & 1975

Factory	Home*	Export*
Birmingham	226	56
Bristol	140	42
Cardiff	175	39
Derby	124	32
Glasgow	250	101
Leeds	121	34
Liverpool	223	86
London	350	122
Manchester	204	66
West Bromwich	172	43

* Figures in thousands.

West Bromwich

(A.L.S.E.B.)

11 Accuracy work and speed tests

Practising the keyboard develops both accuracy and speed, but accuracy is the essential requirement and must not be sacrificed for speed.

Accuracy

After completion, each exercise should be checked for errors. In addition to an obvious mis-typing, errors include:

1	incorrect spacing	–	1	`We goto school.`
2	incorrect punctuation	–	2	`We go to school,`
3	incorrect indentation	–	3	`    We go to school.`
4	a capital letter out of alignment	–	4	`We go to school.`
5	a character not distinctly typed (or typed too heavily).	–	5	`We go to school.`

Measurement of speed

Typing speed is measured at so many words a minute. A 'word' for this purpose consists of 5 strokes or depressions of the keys. Each depression, whether it be a character key or the space bar, counts as one stroke. Thus in a typing line of 60 spaces there are twelve standard words.

Speed can be calculated by dividing the number of words typed by the number of minutes taken. For example, if 200 standard words are typed in 10 minutes, the rate of typing is 20 words a minute. However, for each error made, ten words are deducted as a penalty. Thus if 200 words are typed in 10 minutes, but with 2 errors, the true speed is 200 less 20 equals 180 words which divided by ten equals 18 words a minute.

Exercise 1

Type one copy of the following in double-line spacing on A4 paper. Use a left-hand margin of 50 mm (2 inches) and a right-hand margin of 25 mm (1 inch). Leave a top margin of 25 mm (1 inch).

```
     Slimming has almost replaced the weather as "the"

British topic of conversation.  There is no doubt that the

medical profession has come to believe that overweight

people are more likely to suffer from disease than their

slimmer friends and, as a result, more emphasis is being

placed on diet to prevent ill-health.  In some ways, the

person who puts on weight by over-eating is lucky; he or she
```

EXERCISES

Exercise 1

Type the following table on A5 portrait paper (148 × 210 mm) in double-line spacing. Use blocked style. Centre the table horizontally and vertically, and rule in ink. Leave three spaces between columns.

TREATMENT FOR YOUR HAIR

HAIR STATE	SHAMPOO	SPRAY
DRY	Olive Oil Cream	Spray for dry hair
GREASY	Vitality Lemon	Sunglow for Greasy Hair
VERY DULL	Supercare Herb	Topic Clear

Exercise 2

Type the following table on A5 landscape paper (210 × 148 mm) in double-line spacing. Centre the table horizontally and vertically. Use blocked style. Leave five spaces between columns. Rule up as shown.

Note   As explained on page 132, there is no definite rule about the number of spaces to be left between columns. The aim is to ensure that there is adequate space but, at the same time, the columns are close enough to be ready easily.

If *five* spaces are allocated between columns in a *boxed table with closed sides*, the appearance is improved if the horizontal lines extend *three* spaces (instead of two) beyond the left margin and *three* spaces beyond the last character in the last column. Thus when five spaces are allocated between columns, *three* spaces have to be backspaced from the tab stop.

Giant Supermarkets Limited
Comparison of Total Sales

Division	1982	1983
	£	£
Tinned Foods	1 278 050	1 532 076
Soft Drinks	1 134 098	1 211 654
Farm Produce	742 091	1 011 343
Total	3 154 239	3 755 073

has the extra fat there as a warning sign. Slim people who eat too much are nevertheless subjecting their bodies to the strain of coping with too much food and are also likely to suffer ill-health as a result.

A sensible diet, regular exercise and plenty of fresh air are the ingredients for health.

(W.Y. and L.R.E.B.)

Exercise 2

Type one copy of the following on A5 landscape paper in double-line spacing. Use a left-hand margin of 50 mm (2 inches) and a right-hand margin of 25 mm (1 inch). Leave a top margin of 25 mm (1 inch).

London is the capital city of England. It covers over 700 square miles and has a population of over 8 million.

Every year millions of tourists visit London to see famous places such as Buckingham Palace, The Tower of London, the River Thames and St. Paul's Cathedral. The old city of London (about one square mile in area) is now the commercial centre of Great Britain.

There are so many exciting places to visit - theatres, galleries, concert halls, museums - you need never be bored in London.

(S.W.E.B.)

Exercise 3

Type one copy of the passage in double-line spacing on A4 paper with margins of 40 mm (1½ inches) on the left and 25 mm (1 inch) on the right. Leave a top margin of at least 65 mm (2½ inches).

Photography is a modern miracle, known and used by us all, yet not one person in a thousand ever gives a thought as to how it is all done.

Exercise 3

Type a copy of the following table on A4 paper, taking care with the ruling. Avoid cramping. Used fully blocked style.

SCHEDULES FOR 1978 CHARTER FLIGHTS TO NORTH AMERICA (FROM MANCHESTER)

Destination	Outwards Departure	Return Departure	Departure Periods
Toronto (Canada)	Fridays	Mondays	Mar. 14 to May 31
New York (United States)	Mondays	Sundays	—
New York (United States)	Saturdays	Sundays	May 20 to Sept. 27

(A.L.S.E.B.)

Exercise 4

Type a copy of this tabulation in double-line spacing on A5 paper. Centre your work both vertically and horizontally. Use fully blocked style. Ruling is required.

MOORHEY BUILDING SOCIETY
Table of Calendar Monthly Payments

Loan	10 yrs	15 yrs	20 yrs	25 yrs
£1 000	14.15	11.59	10.47	9.90
£2 000	28.30	23.18	20.93	19.79
£5000	70.75	57.94	52.32	49.48
£10 000	141.50	115.89	104.65	98.95

(L.R.E.B.)

Footnotes

These are used in tabular work and in passages of writing. For example, a footnote inserted at the bottom of a table may be used to explain some detail about the table. In other kinds of work, a footnote may be used to identify the source of a quotation or to provide some further explanation to assist the reader.

The footnote reference is always a superior character. It may be either a figure, or a sign such as an asterisk, dagger or double dagger. In the table or passage, no space is left before the figure or sign. In the actual footnote, one space should separate the figure or sign from the word following. Footnotes are typed in single-line spacing.

In the early part of last century two Frenchmen were at work on the same problem; they had conceived the idea of fixing permanently the little image formed by light in an apparatus they had devised. They joined forces and worked for some time together, until the death of one of them in 1833.

Eventually, the survivor - Louis Daguerre - succeeded in producing photographs on a polished plate of silver by a laborious chemical process, and his wonderful discovery was rewarded by an annuity from the French Government. Several English pioneers, notably Fox Talbot, did much to make photography a practical success.

(W.Y. and L.R.E.B.)

Exercise 4

Type one copy of the following on A5 landscape paper in double-line spacing.

Photography is a very popular hobby. Making photographs is interesting and challenging in all sorts of ways. It is a method of making pictures which does not demand that you be skilled at drawing; a way of commenting on situations which does not require you to be good at words.

Today the range of photographic materials available is vast. Cameras are available the size of matchboxes - some are even attached to radios, very different from the early days when a camera was heavy and a single exposure took several hours.

(S.W.E.B.)

EXERCISES

Exercise 1

Type the following boxed table with open sides on A5 landscape paper (210 × 148 mm) in double-line spacing. Centre the table horizontally and vertically. Leave three spaces between columns. Use blocked style.

LIST OF INSPECTORS

District	Inspector	Assistant
East	Mr A Gibbs	Miss L Tucker
West	Miss V Smith	Mr B Soams
South	Dr L C Brown	Miss G Smart
North	Mrs N Minn	Mr S D Grime

Exercise 2

Type the following boxed table with closed sides on A5 landscape paper (210 × 148 mm) in double-line spacing. Centre the table horizontally and vertically. Leave three spaces between columns. Use blocked style.

LIST OF SCHOOLS

School	Head Teacher	Deputy Head
Fairmead	Mr J Lomas	Mr S Butcher
Swanpool	Mrs V Purchase	Mr G Poole
Coalport	Miss D Saunders	Mr S Jones
Springvale	Mr N Smith	Miss M Peel

Exercise 5
Please type one copy on A4 paper in double-line spacing, of the following passage.

Motorists like to decorate their cars. One of the most common means of decoration is to have a badge or badges on the grille or on the front bumper. Most of these badges indicate that the owner of the vehicle is a member of some of the motoring associations and although there are several of them, the most popular are the Royal Automobile Club and the Automobile Association.

These two organisations provide their members with a variety of services including assistance when buying a second-hand car, insurance for running it and advice on how to run it economically as well as legal advice should this ever become necessary.

Because these organisations are expanding their operations to include non-motoring activities, there is a great deal of concern among members that the organisations are increasing the membership fees but at the same time offering less in the way of motoring services.

(W.J.E.C.)

Exercise 6
Type the following using A5 landscape paper and double-line spacing.

Today we think of a fair as a place where we go to enjoy ourselves. We spend money in the side shows, go for rides on such things as "The Big Dipper" and sometimes have our fortunes told.

Horizontal arrangement

(a) Bring the carriage to the centre point – 30 (pica).

(b) Select the longest line in each column and backspace once for every two letters and spaces in these lines *and* in the spaces to be left between the columns. (Allocate 3 spaces between the columns.)

Note The vertical lines between columns are ruled in the middle of each blank space. Thus in allocating spaces between columns it is best to use an odd number so that there is one for the ruling and an equal number on either side.

There is a total of 9 + 3 + 6 + 3 + 8 + 3 + 6 = 38 spaces and so it is necessary to backspace 19 times.

```
September    Crisps    Biscuits     525.02
   (9)         (6)        (8)         (6)
```

(c) Set left-hand margin at point reached (11).

(d) Set a tab stop for the second column (23); for the third column (32); and for the last column (43).

(e) From the last tab stop tap the space bar once for each character and space in the longest line of the last column (6) *plus two extra spaces* and set the right-hand margin point (50).

(f) Type the main heading and then turn up three lines before returning the carriage to the left-hand margin.

(g) Press margin release key and *backspace two spaces* to give the starting point for the first horizontal line.

(h) Mark the beginning and end of the horizontal line.

(i) Return to the first tab stop (23) and backspace two. Use a pencil to mark the point for the first vertical line. Move to the second tab stop (32) and backspace two. Make a pencil mark for the second vertical line. Move to the third tab stop (43) and backspace two. Make a pencil mark for the third vertical line.

(j) Follow the same procedure and mark points for the vertical lines along the bottom horizontal line.

(k) After removing the paper from the machine, rule the vertical lines before the horizontal lines. This will ensure that the guide marks are not covered up.

If elite type (a width of 70 spaces) is used the left-hand margin is set at 16. Tabular stops are set at 28, 37, and 48. The right-hand margin is set at 56.

Long ago fairs were much more important events. At a
Mop Fair, for example, men and women stood in rows to be
inspected by people who wanted to hire them for farm work or
as maids. Such fairs were called "Mop Fairs" because people
would carry a mop to show they wanted work as cleaners or
would wear a tuft of wool in their hat to show that they
were shepherds. At other fairs the main aim was to sell
animals and so we hear of Goose Fairs or Horse Fairs.

(W.M.E.B.)

QUESTIONS
Write short answers to the following.
1 How is typing speed measured?
2 What makes up a 'word' in speed tests?
3 How many standard words are there in a typing line of (a) 60 spaces, (b) 55 spaces, (c) 50 spaces?
4 State briefly how typing speed is calculated.
5 If 200 standard words are typed in 10 minutes, the rate of typing is _____ words a minute.
6 If the rate of typing is 30 words a minute, how many standard words are typed in 10 minutes?
7 In speed tests, how many 'words' are deducted for each error?
8 If 300 words are typed in 10 minutes but with 2 errors, what is the typing speed?
9 If 200 words are typed in 10 minutes, and the typing speed is judged to be 17 words a minute, how many errors were made?
10 How many words were typed in 10 minutes if the typing speed is 25 words a minute and 5 errors were made?

12 Manuscript Work
Before typing from handwriting, the passage should be read through first to ensure that it is understood.

EXERCISES
Use A4 paper (210 × 297 mm), with a typing line of 60 spaces. Double-line spacing. Make suitable line-end divisions where necessary.

Boxed tables

In this kind of table, there are vertical lines as well as horizontal lines. The sides of a boxed table may be either *open* or *closed* in by vertical lines ruled from the edge of the horizontal lines.

Example

The boxed table with open sides and in blocked style is to be displayed on A5 portrait paper (148 × 210 mm). Type the body of the table in double-line spacing and centre the table vertically and horizontally. Leave three spaces between columns.

TUCK SHOP SALES

(Turn up 3 single lines)

Month	Crisps *(Turn up 2 single lines)*	Biscuits *(Turn up 1 single line)*	Total
	£	£	£
September	50.25	48.39	98.64
October	51.50	47.45	98.90
November	53.48	49.70	103.18
December	30.10	30.20	60.30
January	31.15	29.18	60.33
February	54.12	49.50	103.62
TOTAL	270.60	254.42	525.02

Vertical arrangement

The vertical starting point is found in the usual way, but remembering to count the horizontal lines.

Number of lines on A5 portrait paper = 50
Number of lines and spaces in table = 25
(14 typewritten lines plus 11 blank
lines between the typewritten lines)
Difference to be divided between top
and bottom margins $\overline{25}$
Divide 25 by 2 = 12 (ignore fraction)
Begin typing on line 13.

Exercise 1

Communication means the sending of a message from one person to another. Messages may be transmitted in either written or spoken form.

Written communications include letters, memoranda, reports, telemessages and telex. Spoken messages may be transmitted by telephone and radio.

Modern means of communication assist commerce in three ways. First, information about the state of the market — whether there is an abundance or shortage of a commodity — enables those engaged in commerce to move goods more efficiently to where they are required. Secondly, telephone and telegraph services enable traders to make immediate contact even though they live many miles apart. Finally, the postal system provides a means for the transfer of documents during a business transaction.

Exercise 2

Letters and postcards form the major means of written communication used in the business world. Postcards are used only for messages which are short (such as orders for goods or acknowledgment of receipt)

Exercise 2

Type the following table in blocked style on A5 landscape paper (210 × 148 mm). Use double-line spacing. Centre the table horizontally and vertically, leaving five spaces between the columns.

MONTHLY REPAYMENTS ON MORTGAGES IN £'s

Amount Advanced	20 years	25 years	30 years
1 000	13.40	12.04	11.32
1 500	21.74	17.31	16.84
2 250	32.93	27.09	25.14
5 500	74.01	65.13	60.13

Exercise 3

Type the following table on A5 landscape paper (210 × 148 mm). Use double line spacing and use the underscore for ruling. Centre the table horizontally and vertically and block the headings. Leave five spaces between the columns.

GIANT SUPERMARKETS LIMITED

Sales	1980	1981	1982
	£	£	£
Butter and margarine	894 021	990 000	999 013
Sugar	731 982	844 021	941 029
Tea	2 114 000	2 723 014	2 842 013
Coffee	1 071 642	1 184 023	1 341 024
TOTAL	4 811 645	5 741 058	6 123 079

and not of a private nature.

The telemessage service provides a method of sending urgent messages. A telephone message of up to fifty words may be sent for delivery on the next working day.

Overseas telegrams (usually termed 'cables') may be sent to most parts of the world, to ships in port, to aircraft at airports and to trains at railway stations abroad.

The telex service enables longer messages than could be conveniently sent by telegram to be teleprinted at the receiver's end. Business firms may rent a telex installation from the Post Office. The United Kingdom telex service is fully automatic and immediate connection is made by direct dialling to any subscriber in this country. Similarly, many subscribers abroad may be obtained by direct dialling.

Exercise 3

Most goods sold in shops are branded goods. Manufacturers give their products distinctive names or trade marks which are registered to prevent their use by competitors. Thus, when a person goes shopping she does not simply ask the retailer for a tube of toothpaste, or a packet of washing

Columns of figures
The comma is omitted from columns of figures as follows:

55 073	196 400	1 247 001
1 495	573 750	899 574
342	947 667	3 010 910
99 894	1 401	24 011

EXERCISES

Exercise 1
Type the following table in blocked style on A5 landscape paper (210 × 148 mm).
Use double-line spacing. Centre the table horizontally and vertically. Leave five spaces between the columns.

STOCK RECORDS

Item No.	Description	Purchases	Sales
537	Record Player	7 423	6 400
429	Video Recorder	377	254
706	Television Set	10 749	9 901
836	Transistor Radio	110 721	90 743

powder. Instead she asks for Macleans toothpaste, for Omo or Daz, or one of the other branded tooth pastes and washing powders.

Why do manufacturers brand the goods they make with a distinctive label?

The major reason is that branding makes large-scale advertising possible. If brand names did not exist, a manufacturer of margarine could increase total margarine sales by advertising, but the rise in sales might benefit his competitors as much or possibly more than himself. The use of a distinctive brand name enables a manufacturer to link advertising with his own particular product.

Alterations to manuscripts

Handwritten passages may contain *abbreviations* and *corrections*.

Abbreviations must be typed in full. Some examples are as follows:

Abbreviation	Word in full
a/c	account
amt	amount
co	company
dept	department
exs	expenses
fr	from
pd	paid
recd	received
ref	reference
yr	your

Exercise 2

Type the following table in blocked style on A5 landscape paper (210 × 148 mm) in double-line spacing. Centre horizontally and vertically.

GUIDE CAMP

Guides	Leaders	Helpers
Susan Shaw	Mrs Fraser	Joan Maynard
Helen Round	Mrs Davidson	Margaret Timms
Clare James		
Jean Sloan		
Nita Wedge		

Exercise 3

On A4 paper. Display leaving a blank line between resorts. Type the resorts in alphabetical order.

WESTMID HOLDINGS LIMITED

SAMPLE HOLIDAYS FOR 1979

Resort	Hotel	Month	Price	Nights duration
BINIBECA	Aguamarina	March	£120	7
	Las Vegas	June	£188	14
LLORET	Fenicia	July	£108	7
	Jupiter	August	£145	14
ROVINJ	Lone	May	£150	14
SLIEMA	Delphina	March	£120	7
	Corinthia Palace	October	£152	14
MENORCA	Port Mahon	August	£115	7
RIMINI	Airone	July	£160	14
SINIES	Grand Glyfadu	May	£145	7
HERSSONISSOS	Belvedere	May	£150	7

Ask your local travel agent for further details

(W.M.E.B.)

Type the following exercises. Abbreviations must be typed in full. Use A4 paper (210 × 297 mm) with a typing line of 60 spaces. Double-line spacing. Make suitable line-end divisions where necessary.

Exercise 4

My a/c at Big Homes Building Society shows a balance of £80. Interest is pd fr the time of the first deposit. By this time next yr I should have recd. £10 in interest. Money can be withdrawn on demand except for very large sums. The Society credits interest to a/cs twice during each yr.

Exercise 5

Last week I went for an interview for a Saturday job. The manager was very pleasant and after an interview lasting about 30 minutes, he pd my travelling exs. The manager promised to write to me within a week to let me know whether I had been successful or not. If I get a job, it will mean working in the cosmetics dept. The Co. will write to my head teacher for a ref and I do hope it will be satisfactory.

Exercise 6

Thank you for yr letter which I recd this morning. I was very glad to hear from you. It was interesting to read about your battle with the mail order co. Did the correct gds arrive in the end? You should claim exs for all the trouble you have had. I am sure that a

(b) Select the longest line in each column and backspace once for every two letters and spaces in these lines *and* in the spaces to be left between the columns. (Allocate 5 spaces between the columns.)

There is a total of $13 + 5 + 12 + 5 + 7 = 42$ spaces and so it is necessary to backspace 21 times.

```
The Elephants      Swift Street      Premier
      (13)              (12)            (7)
```

(c) Set left-hand margin at point reached (20)

(d) Set a tab stop for the first column at 38 and for the second column at 55.

(e) From the last tab stop, tap the space bar once for each character and space in the longest line of the column (7) *plus two extra spaces* and set the right-hand margin at that point (64).

(f) Type the main heading and then turn up three single lines before returning the carriage to the left-hand margin.

(g) Press the margin release key and *backspace two spaces* to give the starting point for the first horizontal line. Mark the point either by a light pencil mark or by a light impression of the full stop. Make a similar mark at the right-hand margin.

(h) After the first horizontal line the recommended spacing is *two spaces after* and one space *before* a horizontal line. Mark the beginning and end of each horizontal line.

(i) After removing the paper from the machine, rule up the lines.

If elite type (a width of 100 spaces) is used, the left-hand margin is set at 29. *Tabular* stops are set at 47 and 64. The right-hand margin is set at 73.

EXERCISES

Exercise 1

Type the following table in blocked style on A5 landscape paper (210×148 mm) in double-line spacing. Centre the table horizontally and vertically.

```
SCHOOL CRUISE
```

Children	Teachers	Parents
John Smith	Mrs Rodwell	Mr Grey
Billy Jones	Mr Sims	Mrs Morris
Sandra Brown	Miss James	Mr Allan
Sally Simpson	Miss White	Mr Munro
Jim Green	Mr Young	Mrs Hay

reputable co. would pay a reasonable amt of compensation so let me know what happens after the a/c. has been settled finally.

Margin sign	Text sign	Meaning
Cap or u.c	mary Smith	Capital or upper case letters required
⌒	win⌢dow	Close up – less space between letters or words marked
⋏	⋏	Insert letter, word, or punctuation marks left out. Matter omitted is written in the margin
⌀	windowy	Delete letter or word marked
⊙	⋏	Insert full stop
⊙	⋏	Insert comma
l.c.	winDow	Lower case letters required
		Move to left
		Move to right
NP	[Window	New paragraph
""	⋏	Insert quotation marks
⌐	⌐	Carry straight on – no new paragraph required
#	⋏	Insert space or increase space
stet	school	Let it stand – do not omit words struck out and dotted underneath
trs	Royal Hall Festival	Transpose, i.e. change order of words or letters as marked

Fig. 19 Correction signs

Ruled tables

In this kind of table, horizontal lines are placed (1) above and below the headings and below the last line in the table.

Example

The ruled table in blocked style below is to be displayed on A5 landscape paper (210 × 148 mm). Centre vertically and horizontally and type the body of the table in double-line spacing. Leave 5 spaces between columns.

Note that each horizontal line extends *two* spaces beyond the first and last columns.

RUGBY TEAMS

(Turn up 3 single lines)

| *(Turn up 2 single lines)* | | |
| Name | Ground | League |
(Turn up 1 single line)		
(Turn up 2 single lines)		
The Lions	Roar Road	Premier
The Wolves	Lair Place	First
The Leopards	Swift Street	Second
The Elephants	Lumber Way	First
(Turn up 1 single line)		

Vertical arrangement

The vertical starting point is found in the usual way, but the horizontal lines must be included in the total of lines and spaces in the table.

Number of lines on A5 landscape paper = 35
Number of lines and spaces in table = 16
(9 typewritten lines plus 7 blank lines between the typewritten lines)
Difference to be divided between top and bottom margins $\dfrac{\quad}{19}$

Divide 19 by 2 = 9 (ignore fraction).
Begin typing on line 10.

Horizontal arrangement

The method is the same as in earlier display work with the exception of *setting the right-hand margin.*

(a) Bring the carriage to the centre point – 41 (pica).

Corrections may be in the form of (1) briefly worded instructions and (2) the use of correction signs (Fig. 19). All corrections must be included when a passage is typed.

Type the following exercises, making all necessary corrections. Any abbreviations must be typed in full. Use A4 paper (210 × 297 mm) with a typing line of 60 spaces. Double-line spacing. Make suitable line-end divisions where necessary.

Exercise 7

l.c.

u.c.

each ∧

of

stet

trs

Foreign Trade is the buying and selling of goods between different countries. countries are dependent on ∧ other for supplying their deficiencies in food, food raw materials and machinery. But countries cannot buy the products they need from each other without in selling return. They are also dependent upon each other for markets.

Exercise 8

Of u.c.

wide ∧

run on

N.P.

of N.P.

of

for ∧

l.c.

One way of saving money is to open an a/c with one of the commercial banks the latter provide a ∧ range of services for customers. They are used by businesses and also by private customers. The main types of a/c available are deposit a/cs and current a/cs. [The holder of a deposit a/c receives interest from the bank and money can be withdrawn after giving a short period of notice. this [A current account is one upon which cheeks cheques may be drawn. Cheques are used ∧ making payments to other people and for withdrawals of cash without Notice.

Exercise 5

Type on A5 paper. Use the line-spacing shown. Columns may be blocked as shown or consistently centred.

AZALEAS – NEW VARIETIES

The following varieties *listed below* are offered under numbers as they have not yet been named.

They are available at the exceptionally *each* attractive price of £3.00 as an experimental introduction.

Comments welcomed after a season's flowering.

All are three-year cuttings.

l.c.

NUMBER	Colour	Growth habit
639	Apricot	Tall, open
644	Red	Dense, compact
659	Orange-yellow	Medium
~~718~~	~~Pink-red~~	~~Dense, compact~~
725	White	Tall, open
782	Flame	Medium

Single-line spacing Purchasers will be informed of the names of these varieties in due course.

(N.W.R.E.B.)

30 Ruling of tables

The appearance of a table may sometimes be made more effective by ruling horizontal and/or vertical lines.

In a *ruled* table, the column headings are separated from the column items by horizontal lines.

In a *boxed* table, there are vertical lines as well as horizontal lines.

The simplest way of ruling up a table is with a ballpoint pen or fine felt-tip pen. Pencil ruling is not acceptable.

Exercise 9

l.c. A dept store is a collection of Shops under ⅄ one
roof and the aim is to provide in one building
stet everything ~~that~~ a customer might require.
Caps   william whitley, who built up a huge store
u.c. in london boasted that he could supply ⅄ anything
from a flea to an elephant ⅄. Dept stores still seek
trs to attract shoppers ⌐providing⌐ by opportunities
trs for a many-sided shopping expedition. They sell ⅄
l.c anything from Clothes and Furniture to
l.c Groceries and Pets.

QUESTIONS

Write short answers to the following.

1 What is the first thing to do before starting to type from a handwritten passage?
2 State whether abbreviations in a manuscript should be (a) typed as they appear or (b) typed in full.
3 Write down the word in full for each of these abbreviations.

       a/c   exs   ref
       co   pd   yr

4 Write down the abbreviated form for each of the following.

       amount   from
       department   received

5 State briefly two ways in which a manuscript may be corrected.
6 State the meaning of these correction signs.

7 State which correction signs are used to indicate the following.

       capital letters   new paragraph
       insert a full stop   upper case

8 What is the meaning of (a) stet (b) trs?
9 Which sign is used for insertion of a letter, word or punctuation mark?
10 Write the sign used to mark a deletion in a manuscript.

Exercise 3

Display a corrected copy of this schedule on plain A5. Re-arrange in alphabetical order of employees.

MAXEFIELD ADVERTISING ~~LIMITED~~ AGENCY

caps & underscore — Schedule of Credit Transfers

EMPLOYEE		BANK ~~Branch~~	BRANCH ~~Bank~~	AMOUNT
Fieldhouse	Godfrey	Midton	Selby	£386.50
Granforthe	Gilbert	Westland	Rotherham	£534.00
trs Lindley	Dilys	Doncaster	Doylls	£99.90
Harrison	Anne	Doylls	Doncaster	£99.~~60~~ 90
Hutchison	John	Midton	Selby	£283.30
Spencer	Frank	"	"	£152.25
Rollison	~~Ronard~~ Roland	Westland	Rotherham	£408.30

(Y.R.E.B.)

Exercise 4

Please prepare an unruled layout of this table. Use A5 paper, preferably with the longer side at the top.

AUTO ZOOM LENSES

	MONTAX	PENOLIA	DIXON	PHANTOM CD	DALRYMPLE
35 - 105 mm	£178.34	£180.64	£179.63	£189.41	£182.73
45 - 150 mm	£180.84	£183.14	£182.13	£191.91	£207.98
70 - 210 mm	£190.84	£193.34	£189.13	£195.91	£208.98
70 - 220 mm	£200.00	£293.10	£201.00	£202.22	£210.18
205 mm	£210.82	£300.15	£244.44	£223.12	£230.50
300 mm	£222.30	£342.14	£250.00	£240.50	£231.00

(W.Y. and L.R.E.B.)   Note: CD=compact design

13 Superior, inferior and combination characters

Some characters and special signs require the raising or lowering of the typewriting paper by a small amount. This can be done by a half-space movement of the platen or (if half-line spacing is not provided on a typewriter) by use of the *interliner*.

When this lever is pulled forward, the platen will turn freely. When the interliner is re-engaged, the platen returns to the original typing line. In addition to being used for typing (a) superior and inferior characters and (b) certain combination characters, the interliner is used also for (c) typing double lines underneath totals (see page 140).

Superior (raised) characters

These are characters raised above the normal line of typing. They are typed by turning the paper down half a single-line space, typing the superior character(s) and then returning the platen to the original typing line.

If half-line spacing is not provided on a typewriter, the interliner is used as follows:
(1)   release the platen by means of the interliner lever;
(2)   turn the platen down half a space;
(3)   type superior character(s);
(4)   return interliner to normal position;
(5)   ensure that the platen returns to the original typing line.

Example

Type the following on A5 landscape paper (210 × 148 mm). Use double-line spacing. It is suggested that the example is typed three times.
    Margins: pica 12–72, elite 22–82.

Superior characters are used for typing mathematical formulae such as $Cos^2A + Sin^2A$. They are also used for typing degrees (small o). For example $160\,^{\circ}C$ equals $367\,^{\circ}F$.

Inferior (lowered) characters

These are placed below the normal line of typing. They are typed by turning the paper up half a single-line space, typing the character to be lowered and then returning the platen to the original typing line. If half-line spacing is not provided on a typewriter, then the interliner is used.

Example

Type the following on A5 landscape paper (210 × 148 mm). Use double-line spacing. It is suggested that the example is typed three times.
    Margins: pica 12–72, elite 22–82.

Inferior characters are used for typing chemical symbols such as H_2O; H_2SO_4; CO_2; $C_6H_{12}O_6$ and $CaCO_3$.

4 Use the interliner to turn the platen up slightly and type the double line. Return the interliner to its normal position.

EXERCISES

Exercise 1
Display the following on A5 landscape paper (210 × 148 mm) in double-line spacing. Type horizontal lines with the underscore and use the interliner for double total lines. Leave five spaces between the columns.

£	£	£	£
465.47	97.21	1 071.43	10.44
56.79	86.34	102.57	107.56
947.91	55.45	43.64	948.65
38.13	34.56	84.71	1 949.11
329.35	103.67	75.88	23.02
1 011.57	444.73	56.94	15.04
£2 849.22	£821.96	£1 435.17	£2 053.82

Exercise 2
Display the following on A5 landscape paper (210 × 148 mm) in double-line spacing. Type horizontal lines with the underscore and use the interliner for double total lines. Leave five spaces between the columns.

£	£	£
37.12	108.23	149.22
20.24	411.34	30.34
105.37	306.79	700.43
203.01	244.96	414.79
149.95	10.74	326.98
34.66	15.88	107.00
6.79	37.93	8.40
£557.14	£1135.87	£1737.16

Combination characters

Some characters which are not included on the typewriter keyboard can be made by typing two existing characters in the same space. The first is typed and then, after back-spacing, the second sign is typed over the first.

It is sometimes necessary to use the interliner to allow the characters to be raised or lowered slightly above or below the line of typing. Where half-line spacing is provided on the typewriter, this will often provide the necessary line variation.

A list of combination characters is given below.

Asterisk	Use the small x and hyphen raised half a space	✻
Cent	Use the small or capital c and oblique	¢ ¢
Dagger	Use the capital I and hyphen raised half a space	‡
Division sign	Use the colon and hyphen	÷
Dollar sign	Use the capital S and oblique	$
Double Dagger	Use the capital I raised half a space and another capital I typed slightly below	‡
Equation signs	Use two hyphens, one typed slightly above the other	=
Exclamation Mark	Use the apostrophe and full stop	!
Square brackets	Use the oblique and underscore	⎕

The following are *not* combination characters but are given for information.

Feet	Use the apostrophe after figure(s)	34'
Inches	Use the quotation sign after figure(s)	9"
Minutes	Use the apostrophe after figure(s)	14'
Seconds	Use the quotation sign after figure(s)	30"
Minus	Use the hyphen preceded and followed by one space	4 - 3

55

Note   (1) Figures must be kept in the correct column so that the units, tens, hundreds, etc., are accurately lined up under one another.

(2) The £ sign is blocked at the tab stop set for the longest line.

(3) **If there are more than three digits to the left of the decimal point, use one space to separate groups of three digits, counting from the decimal point.**

Exercise

Type the following on A5 portrait paper (148 × 210 mm). Use double-line spacing and leave five spaces between columns.

£	£	£
314.71	4 378.21	334.74
101.04	1 000.04	491.26
20.76	94.00	1 000.00
288.74	23.76	26.45

Double underlining of totals

In order to type double lines underneath totals of figures, it is necessary to use the interliner.

Example

Display the following table on A5 landscape paper (210 × 148 mm) in double-line spacing. Leave five spaces between the columns. Type horizontal lines with the underscore and use the interliner for double total lines.

£	£	£	£
106.40	1 044.24	72.34	998.74
247.53	13.33	89.48	816.22
589.28	292.49	98.55	75.31
21.00	80.94	146.61	14.11
————	————	————	————
£964.21	£1 431.00	£406.98	£1 904.38
════	════	════	════

Calculate the vertical and horizontal arrangements in the usual way.

Underline as follows, noting that lines should not extend above or below the £ sign.

1 Turn up one single line before typing the first line above the total.

2 Turn up two single lines and type the total.

3 Turn up one single line and type the line below the total.

Multiplication	Use the small x preceded and followed by one space	4 x 3
Brace	Use the opening or closing brackets typed one beneath the other	( ) ( )
Sloping fractions	Use the oblique with no space either side	2/5

Note   A square bracket is typed as follows.

Left bracket: (1) **Type an oblique sign.**

(2) Backspace once and type the underscore.

(3) Turn the platen back one single-line space in order to lower the paper, and type the underscore.

⌐

(4) Turn the platen up one single-line space in order to raise the paper, backspace once and continue with typing up to the right bracket.

Right bracket: (1) **Type an oblique sign.**

(2) Backspace twice and type the underscore.

(3) Turn the platen back one single-line space in order to lower the paper, and type the underscore.

⌐

(4) Turn the platen up one single-line space in order to raise the paper, space once and continue with typing.

EXERCISES

It is recommended that each exercise should be typed at least three times.

Typing line: 60 spaces. Double-line spacing. Make suitable line-end divisions where necessary.

1 HNO_3 is the chemical formula for nitric acid.

2 The asterisk (*) is a star-shaped mark. It is used to mark words for reference or distinction.

3 The cent (¢) is one-hundredth of a dollar ($).

4 A dagger † or a double dagger ‡ may be used to mark foot-notes in a passage of writing.

5 Degrees are units of measurement. For example there are 90° in a right angle.

(c) Set left-hand margin at point reach (15).

(d) Starting from the margin, tap the space bar once for each letter and space of the longest line in the first column. Then tap once for each space between the first and second columns. Set a tab stop for the second column (36).

(e) Continue in the same way and set a tab stop for the third column (52).

(f) Tap the space bar for each letter and space in the final column and check that the two margins are equal.

EXERCISES

Use A5 landscape paper (210 × 148 mm) and type in double-line spacing. Centre vertically and horizontally.

Exercise 1

FORTHCOMING PUBLICATIONS

Name of Author	Subject	Publisher	Date of Publication
B Smith	Commerce	Smith & Son	January
A Jones	Typewriting	D Green Ltd	March
L Brown	Office Practice	V Soap Ltd	May
W Simpson	Accounts	Numerals Ltd	June

Exercise 2

EXAMINATION RESULTS

Name	English	Mathematics	Religious Education
Alan Brown	*Failed*	*Passed*	*Failed*
Joe Grime	*Passed*	*Distinction*	*Distinction*
Liz Williams	*Passed*	*Failed*	*Failed*
Tessa Guest	*Distinction*	*Passed*	*Distinction*
Jim Gaunt	*Failed*	*Failed*	*Passed*

Sums of money in columns

In *blocked style*, sums of money are typed as follows:

£	£
104.30	3 981 000
15.90	424 010
7.45	9 756
0.60	203

6 Which place is situated at 40° North and 18° West on the map?

7 The boiling point of water is 100 °C.

8 60 ÷ 3 = 20; 75 ÷ 5 = 15; 10 ÷ 2 = 5.

9 10 x 2 = 20; 7 x 5 = 35; 9 x 4 = 36.

10 "Hello!", they called. "Can you hear the lark singing?"

11 "Time for sums!" "Please work out the following quickly."

12 120 - 60 ÷ 3 x 2 - 4 x 2 = 450 + 50 - 200 x 2 ÷ 20 + 42

13 $\sqrt{900} ÷ 9 = 100$ $\sqrt{11} x 5 = 55$ $\sqrt{12} ÷ 4 = 3 + 15 - 18 = 0$

14 The apostrophe (') may be used to represent feet, and quotation marks (") may be used to represent inches as, for example, 7' 4" (7 feet 4 inches). The same signs are used to represent minutes (') and seconds (") as, for example, 10' 45" (10 minutes 45 seconds).

15 The brace is a succession of brackets, one below the other, used to link lines together.

(Jean
(Rose
(Audrey

QUESTIONS
Write short answers to the following.
1 State three uses of the interliner.
2 What are superior characters?
3 How are superior characters typed?
4 Give two examples of superior characters.
5 What are inferior characters?
6 How are inferior characters typed?
7 Give an example of an inferior character.
8 What are combination characters?
9 Describe two ways of typing a combination character.
10 Write down nine examples of combination characters.

29 Column headings

In addition to the main heading of a table, there may be a heading for each column. Column headings are usually typed in lower case with initial capitals.

In blocked style, column headings and column items start at the left margin and at the tab stops set for the longest line of each column.

Example

The three columns below are to be displayed in double-line spacing on A5 landscape paper (210 × 148 mm). Centre vertically and horizontally.

CARS FOR SALE

Make	Colour	Year Registered
Ford Granada	Jupiter Red	1979
Mini Clubman	Sunset Red	1977
Peugot 104	White	1978
Opel Manta	Gold	1973
Chrysler Sunbeam	Orange	1976

Vertical arrangement
Number of lines on A5 landscape paper = 35
Number of lines and spaces in table
(7 typewritten lines plus 7 blank
lines between the typewritten lines) = 14

Difference to be divided between top
and bottom margins

$$\frac{35}{-14}$$

$$\overline{21}$$

Divide 21 by 2 = 10 (Ignore fraction)
Begin typing on line 11.

Horizontal arrangement
(a)   Bring the carriage to the centre point – 41 (pica).
(b)   Select the longest line in each column (the length of the column heading must be taken into account in deciding which is the longest line in each column). Backspace one space for every two letters and spaces in these lines *and* in the spaces to be left between the columns. (Allocate 5 spaces between the columns.)
There is a total of 16 + 5 + 11 + 5 + 15 = 52 spaces and so it is necessary to backspace 26 times.

Chrysler Sunbeam	Jupiter Red	Year Registered
(16)	(11)	(15)

138

IV LETTERS, MEMORANDA AND POSTCARDS

14 Addresses

Names in addresses are typed with a space before and after each initial.

Example

```
A L Jones
```

EXERCISES

Type the following names.

1 G K Gnome

2 N N D Salmon

3 V S Lynch

4 A Dyson

5 L A Samuels

Type the following names and titles.

6 Mr G A Tombs

7 Miss V N Glanville

8 Mrs L C Brown

9 Ms M Smith

10 Dr C V Jones

Blocked style

The address shown below is typed in *blocked style*. All lines begin underneath each other.

Example
```
Mr F B Cooper
193 South Street
WESTOWN
WE4 3WN
```

Note   (1)   No commas or full stops are used. This is known as *open punctuation*.

(2)   The address is typed parallel to the longer side of the envelope.

(3)   **The first line of the address appears about half way down the envelope and about 50 mm (two inches) from the left-hand edge on small envelopes, centrally on wider ones.**

(4)   Each part of the address is typed on a separate line.

(5)   The town should be typed in capital letters.

(6)   The postcode is the last item in an address and should be typed on a line by itself.

Exercise 4

Type in double-line spacing, leaving five spaces between columns.

COUNTRIES OF THE WORLD

United States	Russia	China	Turkey
France	Holland	Belgium	Japan
England	Scotland	Peru	Wales
Brazil	India	Mexico	Ireland
Iran	Libya	Pakistan	Canada

Exercise 5

Type in double-line spacing, leaving five spaces between columns. Centre the main heading.

Note on centring the heading.
(a) Move the carriage to the centre point of the paper.
(b) Backspace once for every two letters or spaces in the heading.
(c) Begin typing at the point reached.
(d) Turn up three lines before typing the columns.

TYPES OF FRUIT

Grapes	Strawberries	Pears	Oranges
Raspberries	Lemons	Bananas	Cherries
Plums	Pineapples	Apricots	Damsons
Blackcurrants	Melons	Apples	Peaches

Exercise 6

Type in double-line spacing, leaving five spaces between columns. Centre the main heading.

MERIT AWARDS

Joan Cooper	*Bill Wilson*	*Dennis Payne*
Linda Stephens	*Sandra Jeeson*	*Jean Lawrence*
Elaine Judge	*Helen Knight*	*Bert Disley*
Roy Gee	*Stephanie Hay*	*Henry Forsyth*
Peter Sains	*John Cox*	*Roy Hyman*
Susan Strange	*Ernest Good*	*Andrew Bell*

If this is not possible, then at least two spaces should be left in front of it.

(7) Single-line spacing is used on a small envelope, but with larger envelopes the address may be more easily read if typed in double-line spacing.

(8) Any special instructions such as *PERSONAL*, *CONFIDENTIAL*, *URGENT*, should be typed two lines above the address.

The following examples illustrate some of these points.

```
PERSONAL

Rev P Stevens MA
12 Willow Road
PORTSMOUTH
PR7 8TW
```

```
CONFIDENTIAL

The Headteacher
Churchfold High School
WEST BROMWICH
WB1 2ER
```

longest line in the first column. Then tap once for each space between the first and second columns. Set a tab stop for the second column (32).

(e) Continue in the same way and set a tab stop for the third column (54).

(f) Tap the space bar for each letter and space in the final column and check that the two margins are approximately equal.

EXERCISES

Use A5 landscape paper (210 × 148) and centre vertically and horizontally.

Exercise 1

Type in single-line spacing, leaving five spaces between columns.

```
TOPICS IN COMMERCE

Retailing        Business Ownership       Advertising
Banks            Insurance                Consumer Protection
Transport        Buying and Selling Abroad Wages and Salaries
Communications   Business Records         Payment of Taxes
Wholesaling      Public Ownership         Results of Trading
```

Exercise 2

Type in double spacing, leaving five spaces between columns.

```
OFFICE PRACTICE
```
(Turn up three single lines)
```
Using the Telephone   Written Communications   Petty Cash

Receiving Visitors    Filing                   Reference Books

Mail Handling         Indexing                 Banking

Business Documents    Reprography              Payment of Wages
```

Exercise 3

Type in single-line spacing, leaving five spaces between columns.

```
TOPICS IN TYPEWRITING

Working Parts        Care of the machine    Home Keys
Display Work         Sentences              Personal letters
Horizontal Display   Paragraphs             Circular letters
Postcards            Manuscript work        Tabulation
Minutes              Copy work              Vertical Display
Menus                Business letters       Agendas
Memorandum           Envelope addressing    Notices
```

EXERCISES

Type the following addresses on envelopes in single-line spacing. Use open punctuation. Set the left-hand margin at 20 (pica) or 25 (elite). Turn 14 lines down to begin.

If envelopes are not available for practice in typing addresses, use a sheet of A5 paper folded or cut to half size.

1 Mr N Smith, 36 Flowerpot Grove, Blackpool BL2 5OL

2 Messrs James Bros, 12 Foundry Street, Birmingham B19 3HA

3 The Managing Director, S Stephens & Co Ltd, 3 Ditch Yard, Manchester MA9 3ST

4 The Sales Director, Brown & Black Ltd, Brimstone Works, Grim Way, Wolverhampton WL3 6NS

5 Rt Hon Leslie Brown, Tudor Grange, Royal Avenue, Chepstow CH3 9TO

6 Rev H V Harper MA BSc, The Vicarage, 12 Angel Road, London NW2 7NO

7 Dr S Groaner, The Surgery, Pill Lane, Aberdeen AB9 7EE

8 The Manager, Seaview Hotel, 12 Promenade Way, Southsea SO1 3SE

9 Ms S Dexter, Flat 10, Riverside Court, Stream Road, Leeds LE12 3DS

10 Miss D Salmon, 12 Riches Road, Nottingham NT3 4HA

11 J Denton Esq, 14 Trewlawny Road, Southampton SU9 3PT

12 The Borough Treasurer, Town Hall, Northampton NR3 8PT

15 Personal Letters

The personal letter overleaf (Fig. 20) is typed in single-line spacing on A5 paper (148 × 210 mm) with margins set at 5–55 (pica) or 12–62 (elite). The style is fully blocked.

(*Note*   The use of open punctuation means the omission of commas and full stops except from the body of the letter.)

Exercise 5

A LIST OF COLOURS

blue	red	orange
scarlet	grey	green
pink	white	brown
mauve	bronze	black

28 Horizontal and vertical arrangement

Example
The following table is to be displayed on A5 landscape paper (210 × 148 mm) in single-line spacing.

```
FOOTBALL LEAGUE

Arsenal          Everton              Leeds
Liverpool        Southampton          Wolves
Aston Villa      Manchester United    West Bromwich
Norwich          Sunderland           Bolton
Derby            Newcastle            Barnsley
Brighton         Ipswich              Walsall
```

Vertical arrangement
Number of lines on A5 landscape paper = 35
Number of lines and spaces in table   = 8
Number of unused lines   = 27
Divide by 2 (ignore fraction)   = 13
Type the heading on next line   14
Turn up 2 lines before typing the columns.

Horizontal arrangement
(a) Bring the carriage to the centre point – 41 (pica).
(b) Select the longest line in each column and backspace once for every two letters and spaces in these lines *and* in the spaces to be left between the columns. (Allocate 5 spaces between the columns.) There is a total of 11 + 5 + 17 + 5 + 13 = 51 spaces and so it is necessary to backspace 25 times. (The fraction is ignored.)

```
Aston Villa      Manchester United    West Bromwich
    (11)               (17)               (13)
```

(c) Set left-hand margin at the point reached (16).
(d) Starting from the margin, tap the space bar once for each letter and space of the

135

(Turn up 7 lines)

ADDRESS ———
```
14 Scimitar Street
TEAVILLE
TE7 3LE
```

(Turn up 3 lines)

DATE ———
`2 December 19--`

(Turn up 3 lines)

SALUTATION ———
`Dear Sandra`

(Turn up 2 lines)

BODY OF LETTER
```
I was delighted to hear that you passed your
driving test.  We all send our warmest con-
gratulations.
```
(Turn up 2 lines)
```
It is quite a time since you were over here and I
wondered whether you would like to come to tea on
Friday.  Afterwards we might go dancing or see a
film.
```
(Turn up 2 lines)
```
Do come over if you can.
```
(Turn up 2 lines)
`Sincerely` ——— **COMPLIMENTARY CLOSE**

Fig. 20 The parts of a personal letter

Exercise 2

SCHOOL SUBJECTS

Accounts	Latin	Commerce
Geography	Music	Biology
Home Economics	Physics	History
Italian	Science	Typewriting

Exercise 3

PUPILS ENTERED FOR EXAMINATIONS

Joan Brown	Sheila Allen	Leslie Black
Fiona Davies	Diane Hunt	Mary Graham
John Duncan	George Baugh	Cheryl Gough
Peter Simpson	Dorothy Mills	Ann Round

Exercise 4

EXAMPLES OF CITIES

Liverpool	Birmingham	Manchester
Sheffield	Coventry	Bristol
Brighton	London	Nottingham
Bradford	Southampton	Peterborough

EXERCISES

Exercises 1

Type this example of a personal letter in single-line spacing. Use A5 portrait paper (148 × 210 mm) and set margins at 5–55 (pica) or 12–62 (elite). The spacing is the same as in Fig. 20.

```
50 New Felling Lane
WOLTON
WO4 7NO


8 December 19--


Dear Jean

I am celebrating my fifteenth birthday on Saturday,
18 December with a party at the Community Centre
Hall in Bright Street.  The reason for booking the
Hall (instead of using our front room at home) is
to allow me to invite some of my old friends from
my previous school at Southton plus the new friends
made at Churchfold School since moving here last
August.  Please do join us at 7 pm.

By the way, did you read in the local paper that
John Denton is to play for Southton youth team?
I was in the same form with him before I left the
school.

I do hope you will come to the party.

Best wishes
```

	A4	A5 landscape	A5 portrait
Spaces across the page			
Elite	*100*	*100*	*70*
(centre point of paper)	*50*	*50*	*35*
Pica	*82*	*82*	*59*
(centre point of paper)	*41*	*41*	*30*
Lines down the page			
6 lines to 25 mm (1 inch)			
Elite and pica	*70*	*35*	*50*

Fig. 32 Paper scales

(f) Set left-hand margin at the point reached (15).

(g) Starting from the margin, tap the space bar once for each letter and space of the longest line in the first column. Then tap once for each space between the first and second columns. Set a tab stop for the second column (34).

(h) Continue in the same way and set a tab stop for the third column (51).

(i) Tap the space bar for each letter and space in the final column and check that the two margins are equal.

(j) When typing across the page the tabulator bar is used to jump from column to column.

EXERCISES

Use A5 landscape paper (210 × 148 mm) and type in double-line spacing. Type the heading on the 13th single-line space from the top of the paper and start at the left-hand margin. Turn up 3 lines after the heading. Leave five spaces between columns.

Note (1) Before starting an exercise, move margin stops to extreme left and right and ensure that the left edge of the paper is against the paper guide at 0.

(2) Clear all tab stops.

(3) Type the columns across the page. Do not type one column at a time.

Exercise 1

Scale points for start of columns are given as a guide. Those in brackets are for elite type.

```
STREET NAMES

19 (28)          36 (45)          51 (60)
Abbey Road       Druid Way        Mayfair Way

Adam Street      Essex Road       London Road

Baker Street     Lea Street       Bath Terrace

Bankside         Hall Place       Ivy Street
```

Exercise 2

Type this example of a personal letter in single-line spacing. Use A5 portrait paper (148 × 210 mm) and set margins at 5–55 (pica) or 12–62 (elite).

19 New Road
OLDTOWN
OL3 7WN

2 February 19--

Dear Naomi

I am wondering whether you have made any plans for holidays this summer. Could we go away together? My parents have rented a cottage in Cornwall for the month of August and they say we could have the first two weeks there.

I do hope you like the idea and that you could come in the weeks available.

Hope to hear from you soon.

Yours

VI TABULATION

Tabulation means typing material in table form. In order to make it easy to read and understand the work must be planned out before beginning to type. It should be:

(a) centred horizontally, i.e. equal left and right-hand margins;

(b) centred vertically, i.e. blank paper at top and bottom equal;

(c) arranged so that the columns are evenly spaced and all headings are centred equally one with the other.

27 Horizontal arrangement

Example

The three columns below are to be displayed on A5 landscape paper (210 × 148 mm) in single-line spacing.

```
Alan Jones        Helen Thomas      Stephanie Thomas
Rachel Coulson    Peter Smith       Helen Round
James Simpson     Anne Lomax        Len Peters
Neville Smith     Ivan Gee          Sandra Hodgson
Mary Stott        John Brown        Ian Walters
```

Note   There is no definite rule about the number of spaces to be left between columns. The number selected depends on the width of the table. The aim is to ensure that there is adequate space between columns but, at the same time, the columns are close enough to be read easily. Usually 3 or 5 spaces will be appropriate. In the example, the number chosen is 5.

In order to ensure that the columns are evenly spaced with equal margins at each side, the following steps are required.

(a) Move margin stops to the extreme left and right.

(b) Clear all tab stops.

(c) Insert paper with the left edge at 0 on the paper scale.

(d) Bring the carriage to the centre point of the paper 41 (pica).

(e) Select the longest line in each column and backspace once for every two letters and spaces contained in these lines *and* in the spaces to be left between columns. In the example there is a total of 14 + 5 + 12 + 5 + 16 = 52 spaces and so it is necessary to backspace 26 times.

```
Rachel Coulson   ← 5 →   Helen Thomas   ← 5 →   Stephanie Thomas
     (14)                    (12)                     (16)
```

Ignore an odd character which is left over at the end.

Exercise 3

When writing to a business organisation the address of the organisation is typed on the left, below the date. This is called the *inside address*. In addition, the *writer's name* is typed in case there is difficulty in reading the signature.

Type this example of a *personal-business letter*. Use A5 portrait paper (148 × 210 mm) and set margins at 5–55 (pica) or 12–62 (elite). Turn up five lines to allow space for the signature.

(Turn up 7 lines)

```
34 Canterbury Road
WELHAM
WE9 3MA
```

(Turn up 3 lines)

```
1 May 19--
```

(Turn up 3 lines)

```
The Sales Manager
Castle Garden Nursery
KIDHAM
KI3 6MA
```

(Turn up 3 lines)

```
Dear Sirs
```
(Turn up 2 lines)
```
I have seen an advertisement for your Garden
Furniture Catalogue in yesterday's edition of the
Saturday Advertiser.  Would you send me a copy
please?
```
(Turn up 2 lines)
```
I enclose stamps to the value of 30p as requested
in the advertisement.
```
(Turn up 2 lines)
```
Yours faithfully
```

(Turn up 5 lines)

```
D Spencer (Miss)
```

(Turn up 3 lines)

```
Enc
```

Note   The abbreviation of enclosure (enc) reminds the sender of the letter that an enclosure is to be put into the envelope.

QUESTIONS

Write short answers to the following.

1 What is a meeting?
2 Give three examples of formal meetings.
3 What information is contained in a notice of meeting?
4 A list of items of business for discussion is called an _____.
5 Why is an agenda circulated before a meeting?
6 What are minutes?
7 Who prepares the minutes?
8 Who signs the minutes as a true and fair record?

Exercise 4

Type this example of a personal-business letter. Use A5 portrait paper (148 × 210 mm) and set margins at 5–55 (pica) or 12–62 (elite). Use single-line spacing.

```
18 Manor Street
WOODBRIDGE
WO3 DG9


7 June 19--


Greenline Cruisers Ltd
Canalside Wharf
BRAMPTON
BR6 7OQ


Dear Sirs

Thank you for your letter of 30 May advising me
of a cancellation for the week commencing 2 July.

I accept your offer of the cruiser 'NEW STAR' for
this period and return your booking form duly
completed, together with my cheque for £75.00.

Yours faithfully



Andrea Smith (Miss)
```

Exercise

Type a copy of the following on A4 paper (210 × 297 mm) in blocked style with shoulder headings. Set margins at 10 and 75 (pica), 12 and 90 (elite).

MINUTES of the fifth Annual General Meeting of the Merrytime Social Club held at the Club on Saturday 1 May 19-- at 2 pm.
(Turn up 2 lines)
PRESENT
(Turn up 2 lines)
Mr B Jolly (Chairman)
Mr A Joy (Vice-Chairman)
Mr S Glad
Mrs L Pleasant
Miss V Happy
Mrs D Glee
Mrs B Cheery (Secretary)
(Turn up 2 lines)
1 APOLOGIES

Apologies were received from Mr V Glum and Miss A Woe.

2 MINUTES OF PREVIOUS MEETING

The Secretary read the Minutes of the meeting held on 14 April 19--. These were signed by the Chairman as being a correct record.

3 MATTERS ARISING

There were no matters arising from the Minutes.

4 MEMBERSHIP FEES

It was unanimously decided that the membership fee should be increased by £1 to £5.50.

5 ANNUAL SUMMER OUTING

It was unanimously agreed that the Secretary should make arrangements for an outing to Seaville on Saturday 1 August.

6 DATE OF NEXT MEETING

The date of the next meeting was fixed for Saturday 30 April 19-- at 2 pm.
(Turn up 3 lines)

Chairman _____
(Turn up 2 lines)
Date _____

Exercise 5

Type this example of a personal-business letter. Use A4 paper (148 × 210 mm) and set margins at 12–72 (pica) or 22–82 (elite).

```
7 Labrador Street
BARKING
CA3 17T


9 July 19--


Delicious Dog Foods Ltd
Canine Way
BARKING
DO12 9G


Dear Sirs

I am writing to inform you that a tin of your 'Luscious
Licks' dog food which I bought from Mammoth Supermarkets
was unsatisfactory.

Although the tin had a label stating that it was 'Luscious
Licks' dog food (and claiming that it contained the usual
meat and gravy), it did, in fact, contain a pink-coloured
substance smelling of fish.

I am wondering whether the tin had been incorrectly labelled
because the pink-coloured substance looked like cat food -
probably your well-known brand of 'Pussy Pleasure'.
Certainly my cat, Angela, liked it but my Alsatian dog
(Horatio) refused to eat it and howled mournfully until it
was taken away.

The tin was bought at the branch of Mammoth Supermarkets
in Rover Road.

I await your comments with interest.

Yours faithfully



A Growler (Mrs)
```

Use A4 paper (210 × 297 mm) and type in single-line spacing with double spacing between the numbered items.

MINUTES of an Organising Committee of the Eastbury Tennis Club held at 4 Green Road on 3 December 19-- at 7 pm.
(Turn up 2 lines)
PRESENT
(Turn up 2 lines)
Mr A Racquet (Chairman)
Mr T Ball
Mrs A Court
Mr B Line
Miss O Net (Secretary)

1   Apologies   Apologies for absence were received
                       from Miss N Hardcourt.

2   Minutes   The Minutes of the Meeting held on
                       1 May 19-- were accepted as a true
                       record of the proceedings.

3   Matters arising   There were no matters arising from the
                       Minutes.

4   Working party   The Secretary reported that the working
                       party had completed the work required
                       to the club premises.

5   Annual Dinner   It was agreed that the Secretary should
                       make arrangements for this function to
                       be held at The Wimbledon Hotel on
                       Saturday 3 May.

6   Date of next   It was agreed that the next Committee
    meeting   meeting should be held on 4 April at
                       7 pm.

(Turn up 3 lines)

Chairman _____
(Turn up 2 lines)
Date _____

16 Business Letters

The business letter below in fully blocked style and open punctuation is typed in single-line spacing on A4 paper (210 × 297 mm).

A S WHOLESALE LTD
70 WAREHOUSE ROAD
BIRMINGHAM   B13 4AM
Telephone 021–234–4567

PRINTED HEADING —

(Turn up 3 lines)

REFERENCE — Ref SRT/MJ

(Turn up 3 lines)

DATE — 8 December 19--

(Turn up 3 lines)

INSIDE ADDRESS —
A R Blackwood Esq
Churchfold High School
WEST BROMWICH
WB1 2ER

(Turn up 2 lines)

SALUTATION — Dear Sir

(Turn up 3 lines)

BODY OF LETTER —
Thank you for your letter of 1 December requesting details of our range of crisps and biscuits.
(Turn up 2 lines)
We offer a wide selection of these products and our catalogue and price list is enclosed for your consideration.
(Turn up 2 lines)
I look forward to hearing from you further in due course.

(Turn up 2 lines)

COMPLIMENTARY CLOSE — Yours faithfully

(Turn up 5 lines)

NAME AND TITLE —
Stephanie R Thomas
Sales Director

(Turn up 3 lines)

ENCLOSURE — Enc

Fig. 21 The parts of a business letter

Note   The *reference* contains the initials of the person who dictated the letter (SRT) and those of the typist (MJ).

Exercise 3

Display the following notice of meeting and agenda on A4 paper (210 × 297 mm) in fully blocked style with open punctuation.

The Lingfield Drama Club

A meeting of the Committee of the Lingfield Drama Club will be held in Lingfield Church Hall on 2 May 19 -- at 8 pm.

A G E N D A

1. Apologies 2. Minutes of last meeting 3. Matters arising. 4. Autumn Production 5. Amplification 6. Date of next meeting. 7

6. Any other business

Secretary.

Minutes

The minutes of a meeting are usually typed on A4 paper. The heading contains the name of the organisation, the date, time and place of the meeting and is followed by a list of those present. The items are arranged in the order in which they were discussed and this is usually the order of the agenda. Each item is numbered and may have either a shoulder heading or a side heading. Single-line spacing is employed with double spacing between the numbered items.

Type a copy of the following which is in fully blocked style with side headings. Leave a space of about one inch (25 mm) at the top of the page. Set a tab stop for side headings at 10 (pica) or 12 (elite). Set margins at 32 and 75 (pica) and 34 and 90 (elite).

Although the actual form and style of a business letter will be decided by the organisation sending out the letter, it is important to remember that the basic parts of a letter remain the same.

The use of open punctuation means that in the body of the letter full stops are not required in the following instances:

a   after each initial in a person's name, e.g. `J M Barnwell;`
b   after an abbreviation, e.g. `Mr   Mrs   Co   Bros   Ltd   Messrs   etc.`

Where abbreviations consist of two or more letters the full stops are also left out. No space is left between the letters but one space is left after the group of letters. Some examples are

```
Helen R Thomas MBE MA MP
P Bradshaw Esq MA PhD
am pm
```

In examples of 24-hour clock times 'hours' is abbreviated, e.g. `1450 hrs, 1700 hrs.`

Type a corrected copy of the following.

ALL PALS COMMUNITY CENTRE

Chairman Mr A Glow   9 December 19--

u.c. A meeting of the Social Committee of the All Pals
Community Centre will be held in the Mauve room at the Royal
Hotel on Wednesday 6 January at 7 30 pm.

AGENDA - *spaced caps*

1 Apologies for absence

2 Election of Secretary

5 Correspondence

3 Minutes of last meeting

u.c. 4 Matters arising out of the minutes

6 Progress report by sub-committee on proposed new plumbing
   in the Community Centre

7 Additional cloakroom facilities

8 Any other business

9 Date of next meeting

                                          Ann Goodcheer
                                          Secretary

NOTE TO TYPIST
Numbered items to be
in correct order

127

EXERCISES

Exercise 1

Copy the example of a fully blocked letter with open punctuation. Use A4 paper (210 × 297 mm) and set margins at 12–72 (pica) or 22–82 (elite). Turn up 13 lines to represent the printed name and address of an organisation.

(Turn up 13 lines)

```
Ref  LC/PT
```

(Turn up 3 lines)

```
1 May 19--
```

(Turn up 3 lines)

```
CONFIDENTIAL
```

(Turn up 3 lines)

```
Dust Products Ltd
10 Dry Street
PARCHTOWN     PA3 5WN
```

(Turn up 2 lines)

```
FOR THE ATTENTION OF I STEAM ESQ
```

(Turn up 2 lines)

```
Dear Sirs
```

(Turn up 2 lines)

```
MISS HELEN RACHAEL THOMAS
```

(Turn up 2 lines)

```
Thank you for your letter of 25 April requesting a
confidential report on the suitability of Miss H R Thomas
for the post of secretary.
```

(Turn up 2 lines)

```
During the three years that Miss Thomas has been employed
by this firm she has proved herself to be a first-class
typist.  Her work is neat and careful and she is able to
work on her own initiative.
```

(Turn up 2 lines)

```
This company would be sorry to lose the services of Miss
Thomas, but if her application is successful we should wish
her every success.
```

(Turn up 2 lines)

```
Yours faithfully
BLEEP BOILERS LTD
```

(Turn up 5 lines)

```
L Choker
Personnel Manager
```

EXERCISES

Exercise 1
Type a corrected copy of the following.

HAPPYNIGHT EVENING INSTITUTE

Chairman Major O N Parade   4 June 19--

A meeting of the Advisory Committee of the Happynight
Evening Institute will be held in the Turquoise Room at the
stet Merryday Hotel on Friday 3 July 19-- at 8. pm.
                                                  7

AGENDA — *spaced caps*

1   Apologies for absence

2   Election of Chairman

5   Correspondence

l.c. 3   Minutes of the last Meeting

4   Matters arising out of the Minutes

6   Report of sub/committee on proposed class for flower
    arranging

7   Autumn Dance

8   Any other business

9   Date of next meeting

ROGER ROUGH
SECRETARY

NOTE TO TYPIST
Numbered items to
be in correct order

126

Exercise 2

Copy the example of a fully blocked letter with open punctuation. Use A5 portrait paper (148 × 210 mm) and set margins at 5–55 (pica) or 12–62 (elite). Turn up 10 lines from the top of the paper to represent the printed name and address of the organisation.

(Turn up 10 lines)

Our Ref ARB/NL

(Turn up 3 lines)

15 December 19--

(Turn up 3 lines)

A S Wholesale Ltd
70 Warehouse Road
BIRMINGHAM
BI3 6AM

(Turn up 3 lines)

Dear Sirs
(Turn up 2 lines)
Thank you for sending your catalogue and price list. Unfortunately I quite forgot to ask in my earlier letter for details of your range of canned drinks. Could you supply me with the information please?
(Turn up 2 lines)
Yours faithfully

(Turn up 5 lines)

A R Blackwood
Teacher in charge of the Tuck Shop

Notice of meeting and agenda

When the notice of meeting is sent out, it is customary to include the agenda.

Type a copy of the following which is in fully-blocked style with open punctuation. Use A4 paper (210 × 297 mm) and set margins at 12–72 (pica), 22–82 (elite). Single-line spacing is used for the notice and double-line spacing between the numbered items in the agenda.

```
THE EASTBURY TENNIS CLUB
4 Green Road
NEWTOWN GARDEN CITY

Chairman  Mr A Racquet

20 March 19--

A meeting of the Organising Committee will be held at 7 pm
on Friday 4 April at the above address.

A G E N D A

1  Apologies for absence

2  To consider and approve the minutes of the meeting held
   on 7 January 19-- (Copy enclosed)

3  Matters arising out of the minutes

4  Correspondence

5  Election of representative to Area Championship meeting

6  Any other business

7  Date and time of next meeting


OLIVE NET
SECRETARY
```

Exercise 3

Copy this example of a fully blocked letter with open punctuation. Use A5 portrait paper (148 × 210 mm) and set margins at 5–55 (pica) or 12–62 (elite). Turn up 10 lines from the top of the paper to represent the printed name and address of the organisation.

Ref SRT/MJ

22 December 19--

A R Blackwood Esq
Churchfold High School
WEST BROMWICH
WB1 2ER

Dear Sir

Thank you for your letter of 15 December requesting details of our range of canned drinks.

A catalogue and price list is enclosed for your consideration.

Do not hesitate to contact me if I can be of further assistance.

Yours faithfully

Stephanie R Thomas
Sales Director

Enc

Agenda

Type a copy of the following agenda which is in fully-blocked style with open punctuation. Each agenda item is numbered and typed in single-line spacing with double spacing between items. Use A4 paper (210 × 287 mm) and set margins at 12–72 (pica), and 22–82 (elite).

```
THE CROWNGREEN BOWLS CLUB
43 Woods Road
OLDTOWN

A G E N D A

1   Apologies for absence

2   To consider and approve the minutes of the meeting held
    on 3 December 19-- (Copy enclosed)

3   Matters arising out of the minutes

4   Correspondence

5   Membership fees

6   Any other business

7   Date and time of next meeting
```

(Turn up 3 lines)

```
Ben Mat
Secretary
```

Exercise 4

Copy this example of a fully blocked letter with open punctuation. Use A5 portrait paper (148 × 210 mm) and set margins at 5–55 (pica) or 12–62 (elite).

```
Our Ref ARB/NL


8 January 19--


A S Wholesale Ltd
70 Warehouse Road
BIRMINGHAM
BI3 6AM


Dear Sirs

I have studied your catalogue and wish to place an
order for the following:

10 boxes of plain crisps
15 boxes of cheese and onion flavour crisps
15 boxes of bacon flavour crisps
20 packs of fruit flavour drinks.

Yours faithfully



A R Blackwood
Teacher in charge of the Tuck Shop
```

QUESTIONS

Write short answers to the following.

1 What is an enumeration?
2 State the arabic number equivalent of I, X, C, M.
3 Give the Roman numeral equivalent of 5, 50, 500.
4 State the arabic number equivalent of XX, XL, LXX.
5 Give the Roman numeral equivalent of 25, 60, 82.
6 State two occasions when Roman numerals are followed by a full stop.
7 Give five examples of the use of capital Roman numerals.
8 State two examples of the use of small Roman numerals.
9 In an enumeration, how many spaces are left after a full stop or a closing bracket?

26 Documents for meetings

A meeting is a gathering of people for a particular purpose. A *formal meeting* is conducted according to certain rules, and a written record (called the 'minutes') is made of the events of the meeting. For example, companies and many voluntary associations are required to hold annual general meetings open to all members. In school, staff meetings and meetings of the school council may be organised on formal lines.

Those required to attend a formal meeting must be informed of the date, time and place. Usually this is done by means of a formal *notice of meeting*. The *agenda* is a list of items of business which are to be discussed at a meeting. It is circulated before the meeting in order to give members time to study the items for discussion. *Minutes* are a written summary of the proceedings of a meeting and of the decisions which have been reached. They are prepared by the secretary of the meeting and circulated to the members for approval. It is customary for the minutes to be confirmed by members at the next meeting and then they are signed by the chairman as a true and correct record.

Notice of meeting

Type a copy of the following notice of meeting which is in fully-blocked style with open punctuation. Use A5 landscape paper (210 × 148 mm) and set margins at 12–72 (pica) and 22–82 (elite).

```
THE EASTBURY TENNIS CLUB
4 Green Road
NEWTOWN GARDEN CITY
(Turn up 2 lines)
Chairman  Mr A Racquet
(Turn up 2 lines)
A meeting of the Organising Committee will be held at 7 pm
on Friday 4 April at the above address.  The agenda will be
circulated in due course.
(Turn up 2 lines)
Olive Net
Secretary
```

Exercise 5

Copy this example of a fully blocked letter with open punctuation. Use A5 portrait paper (148 × 210 mm) and set margins at 5–55 (pica) or 12–62 (elite).

Our Ref SRT/MJ

10 January 19--

A R Blackwood Esq
Churchfold High School
WEST BROMWICH
WB1 2ER

Dear Sir

I acknowledge receipt of your order dated 8 January.
Our van will deliver on Thursday morning next and
the driver, Mr Bate, will be pleased to discuss
with you any arrangements that you care to make for
future orders and deliveries.

I trust that we shall be able to be of service to
you for many years to come.

Yours faithfully

Stephanie R Thomas
Sales Director

Exercise 7

With suitable margins, please type a copy of the following.

TIME-SAVING HINTS FOR THE BUSY TYPIST → *Centre*

Frs The following ~~useful~~ *two* techniques will need a little practice but once mastered they are effective time-savers.

1. Typing near the bottom of the page

    The paper tends to slip if typing is carried on into the bottom inch of the paper. To avoid this adopt the following procedure:

    (i) Feed the top copy, carbon paper and under copy into the machine in the usual way.

    Typist: block all paragraphs as shown → in (i)

    (ii) Insert an extra sheet of paper between the bottom of the top copy and the bottom of the carbon paper. Be sure you know which is the top copy. The extra sheet will be between the reverse side of this and the uncoated side of the carbon paper.

    (iii) This extra sheet of paper holds the copies firmly in place and you will now be able to type to the bottom of the page.

2. Additional typing on carbon copies only

    Carbon copies may require additions which are not wanted on the top copy. This can be achieved by proceeding as follows: *(without removing the carbon copy from the machine)*

    (i) When the material has been typed, turn the paper back until about ② inches show above the card holder. *use the word*

    (ii) Take hold of the bottom of the carbon copy and place this between the top copy and the carbon paper.

    (iv) ~~(iii)~~ Turn the platen to the position necessary for the additional material to be typed on this carbon copy.

    (iii) Roll the platen backward. This will release the top copy and the carbon paper, and draw the bottom of the carbon copy down into the typewriter.

(N.W.R.E.B.)

122

Exercise 6

Type the example of a fully blocked letter with open punctuation. Use A5 paper (148 × 210 mm) and set margins at 12–62 (elite) or 5–55 (pica). Make your own line-endings.

Note   **1**   *Attention line*   Where there is a rule that all correspondence must be addressed to the firm or organisation and not to individuals, it is common practice to insert an attention line.

2   *Subject heading*   This may be used to provide a useful quick description of the contents of the letter.

If typed in lower case any subject heading is usually underlined.

Ref ARB/NL

9 March 19--

Westshire Potato Products Ltd
900 Commercial Street
NEWTOWN
Westshire
WE3 9SE
(Turn up 2 lines)
For the attention of Mr Sid Tuber
(Turn up 2 lines)
Dear Sirs
(Turn up 2 lines)
Order Number LT 34
(Turn up 2 lines)
I regret to inform you that three cases of potato crisps delivered to the school on 8 March were unsealed. When the cases were examined, six packets were missing from the first case; twelve were missing from the second case; and in the third case there were no packets at all.

Your early attention to this matter would be appreciated.

Yours faithfully

A R Blackwood
Teacher in charge of the Tuck Shop

Exercise 5

(a) The list of kings includes Edward VII, George VI, James I, Charles II and Henry VIII.

(b) In support of his argument, the judge read from the Firearms Act 1980, Section N, Sub-section ix.

Exercise 6

Reports

A report is a written statement prepared by a person, or group of persons. It may be brief or extend to many pages.

In a long report, headings and sub-headings are used to divide the report into sections. Each section is lettered or numbered to allow the reader to find quickly any part of the report which is of particular interest. There are a number of methods of numbering and lettering sections, but an example of one widely used method is given below.

I Section	(Roman numeral)
1. Paragraph	(Arabic figure)
(a) Sub-paragraph	(lower case letter)
(b) Sub-paragraph	(lower case letter)
2. Paragraph	

Exercise 7

Type the example of a fully blocked letter with open punctuation. Use A4 paper (210 × 297 mm) and set margins at 22–82 (elite) or 12–72 (pica). Turn up 13 single lines from the top of the paper to represent the printed name and address of an organisation.

Ref ST/OG

12 March 19--

The Head Teacher
Churchfold High School
WEST BROMWICH
WB1 2ER

FOR THE ATTENTION OF MR A R BLACKWOOD

Dear Sir

Order Number LT 34

I have received your letter of 9 March in which you state that three cases of potato crisps were unsealed and part of the contents were missing.

The matter has been investigated and it appears that the cases were broken into while the van driver was making a delivery to another school.

I apologise most sincerely for this unfortunate incident and a new supply of crisps will be delivered today.

Yours faithfully
WESTSHIRE POTATO PRODUCTS LTD

Sid Tuber
Sales Manager

Uses of Roman numerals

1   In tabular work, e.g. Table IX
2   In numbering chapters and headings, e.g. Chapter XV
3   To designate monarchs, e.g. Elizabeth II
4   For numbering school forms or classes, e.g. Form III, Class IIA
5   For a year, e.g. 1957 = MCMLVII
6   *Small* Roman numerals – i, ii, iii, iv.... are used for
    (a) numbering of pages in the preface of a book, e.g. page v
    (b) numbering sub-paragraphs or sub-sections, e.g. sub-section ix,
        paragraph 3 (ii).

EXERCISES

Exercise 1
Type the list of Arabic and Roman numerals given on page 119.

Exercise 2
Type the section headed *Uses of Roman numerals* above.

Exercises 3–6
Type the following exercises on A5 landscape paper (210 × 148 mm) in double-line
spacing. Set margins at 12–72 (pica) or 20–80 (elite).
Note   When lines or paragraphs are numbered or lettered, two spaces are left after
a full stop, number or a closing bracket.

Exercise 3

1.   Everyone in Year VI and Year VII will take Stage III of

     the examination.

2.   Read for homework tonight Chapter X, Chapter XV and

     Chapter XXV.

Exercise 4

(1) Study Tables IV and VIII before writing up the

     experiment.

(2) Turn to page 40 and study Section IX, sub-sections

     (i), (ii) and (iii).

Exercise 8

Type the following letter in fully blocked style with open punctuation. Use A4 paper (210 × 297 mm) and set margins at 22–82 (elite) or 12–72 (pica). Turn up 13 single lines from the top of the paper to represent the printed name and address of an organisation.

Our Ref BB/TW   Insert today's date.

Mrs L Newton 43 Red Road Oldtown OL4 3WN

Dear Madam

Car Repair No L93/4

We were extremely sorry to learn from yr letter that while driving away from here after collecting your car from our service dept, both front wheels fell off the car. [The mechanic who did the repair to the front wheels is convinced that the wheel nuts were tightened up before the car left the workshop. Nevertheless we are very concerned when something like this happens and Could you contact the service manager, Mr Joe Greaser, who will arrange for the car to be inspected at your convenience.

Yrs ffy   B BLUSTER   MANAGING DIRECTOR

Exercise 9

Type the following letter in fully blocked style with open punctuation. Use A4 paper (210 × 297 mm) and set margins at 22–82 (elite) or 12–72 (pica).

Ref MMS/OT   Insert today's date

Mr H I Jack 100 Songster Street Nashtown NA2 WN3

Dear Mr Jack I was delighted to receive your request for a signed photograph of our new sensational Rock Group, the Magnificent Mouths. Unfortunately for you, the incredible demand for these superb pictures has cleaned out the initial order for half a million please be patient with us and we wish will rush a copy to you as soon as new stocks arrive. Meanwhile I expect you know that the Magnificent Mouths start their nation-wide tour next week, taking in twenty major towns and cities throughout Britain.

See you there!

Yours sincerely

MAURICE M SMOKER
Tour Executive

Some examples of Roman numerals are as follows:

Arabic	Capital Roman	Small Roman	Arabic	Capital Roman	Small Roman
1	I	i	20	XX	xx
2	II	ii	25	XXV	xxv
3	III	iii	30	XXX	xxx
4	IV	iv	40	XL	xl
5	V	v	50	L	l
6	VI	vi	60	LX	lx
7	VII	vii	70	LXX	lxx
8	VIII	viii	80	LXXX	lxxx
9	IX	ix	82	LXXXII	lxxxii
10	X	x	90	XC	xc
11	XI	xi	100	C	c
			111	CXI	cxi
			500	D	d
			536	DXXXVI	dxxxvi
			1000	M	m

Note (1) When typing a column of numerals, line up the right-hand figures under each other i.e. blocked right. Use the back spacer where necessary.

```
        I              i
       II             ii
      III            iii
```

(2) Roman numerals are only followed by a full stop at the end of a sentence or when numbering paragraphs.

Exercise 10

Type the following letter on a sheet of A4 paper (210 × 297 mm). Turn up a *minimum* of 7 single line spaces at the top of the paper before beginning to type. Date the letter   22 May 19—

Tel No 0532 69722

Longtoft
Eight Acre Lane
LEEDS
LS9 7FE

T G Porter Esq MSc
Hilton Lodge
HESSLE
North Humberside
HU13 OPT

Dear Sir

Dr White of The Vicarage, Hessle, has suggested that I write to you about a series of books I am planning.

The overall theme of the series will be children's pets and each book will deal with a different animal. There will be a brief history of the development of the animal - see enclosed specimen page on Poodles - and sections on care, exercise, and especially on the suitability of the animal as a pet. The books are intended for young people and they will be written in simple language and well illustrated.

Having read your recent articles on animal welfare, I wonder whether you would be interested in contributing any material for this series. If you are, perhaps we could arrange a meeting in the near future to discuss the matter.

Yours faithfully

Peter Winter

Enc 1

(W.M.E.B.)

QUESTIONS

Write short answers to the following:

1 A _____ heading is used to give the title or subject of a passage of writing.
2 State the spacing to be allowed between spaced capital letters.
3 A heading used underneath a main heading is called a _____ heading.
4 With a _____ heading the text begins on the same line as the heading.
5 A _____ heading is begun at the left-hand margin and is separated from the material below by one blank line.
6 A _____ heading is typed inside the left-hand margin.
7 A side heading may be known also as a _____ heading.

25 Paragraph divisions and sub-divisions

Lettering and numbering

An *enumeration* is a set of paragraphs or lines which are either lettered or numbered. In a letter, for example, information may be displayed by numbering or lettering particular items. Again, in a written statement (such as a report) where headings and sub-headings divide the statement into sections, each section may be lettered or numbered. The purpose is to assist the reader to find quickly any part of the statement which is of particular interest.

Numbering may involve the use of large or small Roman numerals.

Roman numerals

Roman numerals are compiled from the following letters:

Roman	Arabic
I	1
V	5
X	10
L	50
C	100
D	500
M	1000

A letter placed *before* one of greater value indicates that the first is subtracted from the second to find the sum, e.g. XC = 90.

A letter placed *after* one of greater value indicates that both are added to find the sum, e.g. LX = 60.

118

QUESTIONS

Write short answers to the following.

1 What information is contained in a printed letter heading?
2 In the reference ALL/SMT, which initials represent (a) the writer, (b) the typist?
3 The form of greeting at the start of a letter is known as the ＿＿＿＿＿＿＿.
4 Which part of a letter contains the writer's message?
5 Why is the writer's name typed underneath the personal signature?
6 What other information should be typed just below the writer's name?
7 (a) What does the abbreviation 'Enc' mean? (b) What does it indicate?
8 Describe briefly the fully blocked style.
9 How is the form and style of a business letter determined?

17 Copying and correcting

Carbon Copying

It is usual for an organisation to keep copies of documents that are sent out. For this purpose the typist uses carbon paper.

In preparing to take carbon copies:

1 *The coated side of the carbon paper is placed face down on to the paper on which the copy is to be made. (Fig. 22)*
2 *The paper on which the original (ie the top copy) will be typed is then placed over the back of the carbon sheet.*
3 *If additional copies are required, the procedure is repeated.*

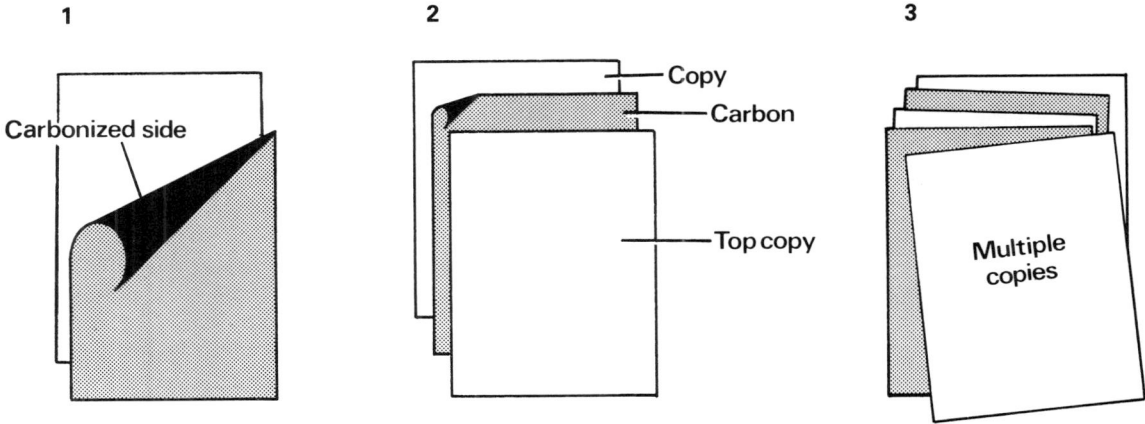

Fig. 22 Taking carbon copies

When the sheets are inserted in the machine, care should be taken to ensure that (a) the coated side of the carbon paper faces the platen and (b) the feed rollers grip all sheets at the same time.

Exercise 5

Correct the following extract on an A4 sheet, in double-line spacing. Use equal margins.

TOURING HOLIDAY BY SEA — *centre!*

STARTING POINT   Start any day you like and travel here to Ireland by any one of the ferry routes of your choice. *sea* There are four routes to choose from and detailed schedules are shown on our 1978 traveller's card.

stet
u.c.

OUR HOTELS   The ~~five~~ three 'Johnson' hotels situated on the western coastline are ideally located for touring the most beautiful parts of the

u.c.

country. The choice of an Itinerary is yours and you can pick any combination of nights at the ~~three~~

stet

~~five~~ hotels covering the full duration of your holiday.

STOPOVERS   To help you plan a leisurely itinerary, stopovers are permitted for one night at the beginning or end of your holiday at the port

trs

of departure or entry - at a small supplementary charge.

TOUR NO 388M   Your price includes car ferry travel with return ticket for passenger and car of any length on the sea route of your choice; hotel accommodation for six nights in room with private bath, and full breakfast. When 4 or 5 adults travel in the same car, a reduction of £7 per person is given.

MIDWEEK TRAVEL   If you travel with your car to and from Ireland on a Monday, Tuesday, Wednesday or Thursday (day or night), we will deduct £15 from your account.

You choose the hotels at time of booking.

(A.L.S.E.B.)

Corrections on top copies

Typing errors may be corrected by use of a rubber eraser as follows:

(1) Turn up the paper so that the mistake is on top of the platen.

(2) Move the carriage to the extreme left or extreme right, according to the position of the erasure, so that the dust falls on the desk and not in the type basket (Fig. 23).

Never overtype it8s quite unaxceptable

mistakes must be erased
and corrected properly

TYPING MUST BE PERFECT

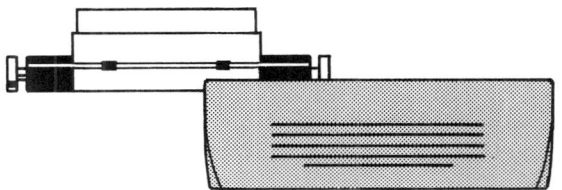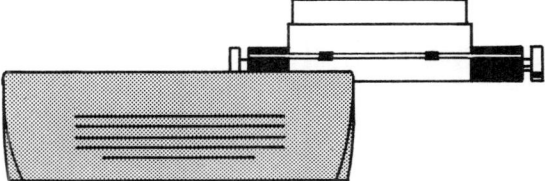

Fig. 23 Correcting errors

(3) Press the paper firmly against the platen to prevent it slipping.

(4) Rub *gently* with the eraser in order to avoid making a hole in the paper.

(5) Turn the paper back to the typing line and type the correction.

Other types of eraser are available (e.g. correction paper or correction liquid) but the procedure for locating the error for correction and returning the carriage for typing, is the same as above.

Overtyping, that is typing the correct characters over mistakes without first erasing them, must never be done. The result is untidy and messy.

Corrections on carbon copies

In order to avoid producing a smudge on the carbon copy:

(1) Insert a piece of card or paper between the carbon paper and the carbon copy.

(2) Erase the mistake on the top copy.

(3) Lift the carbon paper, remove the piece of card or paper and erase the mistake from the carbon copy.

(4) Type the correction.

If more than one carbon copy is being made, then a piece of card or paper should be inserted between each sheet of carbon paper and carbon copy. This enables mistakes to be erased on all carbon copies.

Exercise 4
With suitable margins, please type a copy of the following.

REDIRECTION OF CORRESPONDENCE

If you are moving, you may want to arrange to have your mail redirected to your new address. There are two types of redirection, known as private and official.

1. Private redirection

Mail can be redirected for you by someone at the old address, by deleting the old address, inserting the new one, and re-posting. If an adhesive label is used for the purpose of indicating the new address, the name of the addressee must not be obscured, otherwise the packet will be liable to surcharge. No extra charge is made for the private redirection of letters if they are re-posted not later than the day after delivery and have not been tampered with.

2. Official redirection by the Post Office

The Post Office will normally undertake to redirect your mail. All you have to do is complete a form which can be obtained at any Post Office, and hand it in or send it with the appropriate fee to the Head Post Office serving your old address. You should give at least seven days' notice before you want redirection to start.

3. Fees

The appropriate fee and the period of redirection can be obtained upon application to any Post Office. A separate fee is payable for each different surname. Additional postage may be payable when letters are redirected abroad.

4. Parcels

A charge equal to the original postage is generally payable on redirected parcels.

(W.J.E.C.)

EXERCISES

Exercise 1

Type this letter using A4 paper. The reference is Ref BM/AT and the date is 16 January 19––. The name and address is Miss M Sambrook 34 Green Lane Wolverhampton WV3 5RR. Take a carbon copy.

Dear Miss Sambrook

ISLAND HOLIDAYS IN THE MEDITERRANEAN

Thank you for your letter dated 2 January in which you asked for advice about island holidays during peak season in the Mediterranean. I would suggest that you consider Corfu or Malta - details are to be found on pages 34-41 and 95-99 of the enclosed booklet. For your further information I offer the following.

The island of Corfu is Greek owned and lies off the west coast of Greece. It is aptly named the 'Gateway to Greece' and is an ideal island for both the holiday-maker who wants to get away from it all and the one who wants to go sightseeing. Flights leave Birmingham every Wednesday at 1300 hrs during the season.

Malta lies at the very heart of the Mediterranean and has the added advantage that English is spoken practically everywhere on the island. On an island only 17 miles by 9 you are never far from the sea and with car hire at around £6.50 a day you can afford to see all the sights. Flights leave Birmingham every Tuesday at 2100 hrs or East Midlands Airport every Thursday at the same time.

I have taken the liberty of sending you a booking form and our Holiday Information sheet. If I can be of further assistance, please do not hesitate to contact me or consult your local travel agent.

Yours sincerely

Brian Martin

ENCS

Typist! Please address an envelope for this letter

(W.M.E.B.)

80

Exercise 3
Type a corrected copy of the following. Use double-line spacing.

CARBON COPYING — *spaced caps*

CONTINUOUS STATIONERY ⟶ *centre and underscore*

Typing carbon copies can be a lengthy process.

stet However, time can be ~~saved~~ *gained* by the use of continuous

stationery. Sets of forms are fastened together

ready for typing and each set is also attached [the]²

trs to¹ next one. Thus there is a long continuous strip

of stationery and once the first set has been

inserted in the typewriter, there is no more

insertion to be done as each set follows on. Each

set is divided from the other by perforations/to *NP*

assist easy separation after typing.

shoulder heading ⟵ OBTAINING COPIES

Copies are obtained in a variety of ways. For

l.c. example, the Sets of documents may be interleaved by

the manufacturer with sheets of 'one time' carbon

c/ paper. As the name suggests, this quality of carbon

is intended for use once only and is thrown away

when typing has been completed. The documents may

trs be²/also¹ supplied with a carbon backing so that

separate carbon paper is not required. When the top

NP copy of the set is completed/a copy or copies are

automatically produced beneath it.

Exercise 2

Type a correct version of the letter below on A4 paper. Take a carbon copy. Use fully blocked layout with open punctuation and today's date.

Our ref CSR/78

Mr D Beeden
18 Manor Road
WOODBRIDGE
WO4 8BR

Dear ~~Sir~~ Mr Beeden

Thank you for your letter of 17 May returning the completed booking form in respect of our cruiser "Belle Marie".

We are pleased to confirm this booking for six people for 1 wk commencing 2 September and acknowledge with thanks receipt of your cheque for £38.00. We will write to you again in August with the hire invoice & full directions of how to reach our wharf at Burnholme.

NP/ [In the meantime, we are enclosing a list of the books available concerning the Shropshire Union canal which we think you might find useful.

run on/ If you wish, we can arrange to have fresh milk, eggs, & general groceries on board your cruiser awaiting your arrival.

Yours ~~faithfully~~ sincerely
REDELINE CRUISERS LTD

C S Rede

Enc

(Y.R.E.B.)

81

Exercise 2

Correct the following notice and type in double spacing except for the Food Guide entry which should be typed in single spacing.

THE PREMIER HOTEL

The Premier Hotel offers a golden welcome to the ~~south~~
Skt ~~north~~. Each suite has its own patio, with a
trs magnificent view of the ⌐countryside⌐ surrounding⌐.
They are ideally suited for long or short visits.
Every one of the 125 bedrooms is fully equipped to

All rooms are fitted with radio, telephone and intercom.

modern luxury standards⌐. ~~With restful fine colour~~
~~schemes, radio, telephone and television at hand, a~~
~~Premier bedroom makes comfortable headquarters for a~~
~~business or private stay.~~

N.P. ⌐CONFERENCE ROOM   The Mancunian Room⌐ has every   ♂⌐
convenience for the seating and catering for up to

stet ~~200~~ ~~300~~ persons. Adjoining is a special banqueting
room. Coffee and tea are served from side tables.

NP. ⌐RESTAURANT   The Hotel has a fine restaurant, as is
made clear from the following special entry in the

u.c. current traveller's food guide:

"Christine and John Miller run a dignified
restaurant at the Premier Hotel. ~~with windows~~
~~looking out over the lawns and meadows round~~
~~this grand house.~~⌐ The fresh foods are carefully
cooked by Mr Miller, who clearly runs an
orderly kitchen. ~~His dishes are well presented~~
~~and have plenty of flavour.~~ The set lunch menu
features mainly ⌐ items."   *traditional*

Mrs Miller helps guests choose from a neat handwritten menu, which is well balanced and offers some interesting seasonal items.

NP ⌐Gratuities are ~~always~~ left to the discretion of the ♂⌐
guest, except where a prior arrangement has been
made. Credit Card facilities are available. The
new manager will gladly give details.

(L.C.C.)

Exercise 3

Type a correct version of the letter below on A4 paper. Take a carbon paper copy. Date the letter for 12 January 19–– and address it to Mr R J Sunley BSc of Maxefield Advertising Agency 77a Greensett Place London SW16 5DY. The reference is S/FW/BB

Dear Mr Sunley

SUMMER 1979 PROMOTION

NP/ As requested, I am forwarding to you under separate cover two of the sample containers which The Yorkshire Glass Co. have submitted for final approval for use with our new range. [Your recommendation of Yorks. Glass was well founded — we are delighted
S/ with that the design & quality of their products proved and the prices & delivery date they have quoted.

preferred I must admit that I wd have (prefferred) the closure on the 57 g jar to be of the same flecked gold finish as that on the 25 ml bottle, but the price quoted for the special run-off involved would not be economic from our point of view.

u.c./ Our marketing Dept. is scrutinising the sales figures of the retail outlets / already stocking our products & will send you an updated list in a few days' time. We can / include discussion of the implications of these figures when we all meet
s/et/ next Thurs. to decide view upon the art work for this promotion.
Yrs faithfully sincerely
CHARISMA COSMETICS LTD

Sales Manager

(Y.R.E.B.)

82

contains a set of printed forms and when one of these is properly filled in, it becomes the customer's instruction to the bank.

LOANS   A large number and wide variety of customers borrow from the commercial banks. Most of the banks' lending is to businesses but substantial amounts are also lent to public authorities - local councils, government departments and nationalised industries - and to private customers.

EXERCISES

Exercise 1

Type a copy of the following on A4 paper (210 × 297 mm).

<u>METHODS OF COMMUNICATION</u>

<u>RADIO TELEPHONE</u>

Public mobile radio telephone services are in operation in the London area and in several other regions. Subscribers with suitably equipped vehicles within the areas covered can have calls to or from any telephone within the United Kingdom.

<u>RADIO</u>

Radio is used as a method of communication by the police, the fire brigade, taxi-cab companies and many others. Radio stations broadcast regular weather bulletins to aid ships at sea, and road reports to assist drivers to avoid areas of heavy traffic congestion.

<u>CONFRAVISION</u>

British Telecom has opened television studios in various major cities which can be used for business conferences. Groups of people in different cities are able to conduct meetings as though they were all in the same room. The television link permits face-to-face meetings between people without the inconvenience of long-distance travel.

Exercise 4

Type the following letter using the reference FLPT/W/78/1 and today's date. Take a carbon copy.

(J) Miss ~~M~~ Dyson
Honorary Secretary
Kempton Society (CH5 6AW)
65 Mold Street
~~MMM~~ CHESTER

Dear Madam

(at this hotel)   (accommodation)

Thank you for your letter about the meeting facilities

NP/ we can offer. [I am ~~happy~~ pleased to enclose
our recently-prepared illustrated leaflet and tariff.

NP/ [Although we have no Conference Room reservations
on any one of the autumn dates you mention, we
are at a loss to understand your needs from
~~xxxxxxxxxxxxxxxxxxx~~ the information provided.
Presumably a number of your members will require
overnight accommodation and some might even
wish to prolong their stay in this area.

NP/ [I hope we shall be able to welcome ~~xxxxxxx~~ your
Society to the Premier and look forward to a further
letter from you.

Yours faithfully

Manager

(L.C.C.)

83

Side headings

This form of heading (known also as a marginal heading) is typed inside the left-hand margin, usually in closed capitals. The use of the underscore is optional.

Side headings may be arranged as follows.

(a)   Decide on left and right margins.

(b)   Set the right-hand margin.

(c)   Set a tab stop at the point where the side headings begin.

(d)   Add up the number of letters and spaces in the *longest* of the side headings and add 3 extra spaces.

(e)   Add the total above (d) to the number set by the tab stop at the point where the side headings begin (c).

Set the left-hand margin at this total, i.e. where the lines of text will begin.

(f)   Use the margin release key to start typing the side headings at the point set by the tab stop (c).

Example g

Type the following on A4 paper (210 × 297 mm) using single-line spacing with double-line spacing between the blocked paragraphs. Use side or marginal headings as shown.

Note   (1)   Right-hand margin is set at 75 (pica), 85 (elite).

(2)   Tab stop set at 10 (pica), 20 (elite).

(3)   Number of letters and spaces in the longest side heading ('Statement') = 9 plus 3 = 12.

(4)   Left-hand margin is set at 12 + 10 = 22 (pica)

12 + 20 = 32 (elite).

<u>BANKING TERMS</u>

(Turn up 3 lines)

DEPOSITS   Commercial bank deposits are a convenient way of holding savings. Deposits can be made in either a current account or a deposit account, or in both. There is also a third type of account known as a savings account.

STATEMENT   The bank keeps a record of every payment made into, and every withdrawal out of a current account. These records are maintained on ledger sheets showing the day-to-day balance. The bank issues an exact copy of this (the bank statement) at regular intervals.

CHEQUES   The current account depositor receives a cheque book which is used both to make payments to others and to withdraw cash. A cheque book

112

QUESTIONS

Write short answers to the following.

1 State briefly how the original, copy and carbon papers are arranged for typing a copy.
2 During typing, does the coated side of the carbon paper face the platen or face away from the platen?
3 Give another point to check when inserting the papers in the machine.
4 When a mistake is rubbed out, how is the paper positioned on the platen?
5 Why is the carriage moved to the extreme right or left when erasing?
6 What might happen if the eraser is not used carefully?
7 (a) Name other methods of correction available in addition to a rubber eraser.
   (b) Describe briefly how each is used.
8 What is 'overtyping'?
9 Why should overtyping never be used as a method of correction?
10 Why is it necessary to shield a carbon copy when erasing on the original?
11 How can the carbon copy be protected?

18 Memoranda

A memorandum (generally referred to briefly as a *memo*) is used for communication within an organisation.

It may be typed on any of the standard sizes of paper but the most usual is A5 landscape paper (210 × 148 mm). An example is given in Fig. 24.

Printed memorandum forms

MEMORANDUM

FROM: A Royle   TO: Miss J Shaw

REF: AR/SL   DATE: 12 May 19--

School Play

Please express my gratitude and thanks to the typists in Form
5C1 for their help in producing the school magazine. Their work
is of a very pleasing standard.

Fig. 24 Memorandum on a printed form

INSURANCE

     Insurance provides compensation for damage to, or loss
of, goods and raw materials.

ADVERTISING

     Advertising provides consumers with information about
goods available for sale. Advertising assists, therefore,
in the selling of goods.

Example f

Type a copy of the following on A4 paper (210 × 297 mm) using blocked paragraphs
and single-line spacing. Centre the main heading on the typing line. Set margins at
12–72 (pica), 22–82 (elite).

RECORDING TRANSACTIONS

In the business world, the buying and selling of goods and
services is done usually on credit, that is, goods are
dispatched by the supplier in advance of payment by the
buyer. Each transaction is recorded by a series of documents
showing value received by the buyer and the amount owing by
the supplier.

REQUISITION

In a large organisation, the purchasing department is
responsible for buying goods required for use in the
business. Hence requests from other departments for goods to
be purchased are sent to this department and a requisition
is prepared.

QUOTATION

This provides all the information required by the buyer
including prices; terms of payment (or settlement), the
period of delivery; and the terms of delivery.

ORDER

The purpose of an order is to provide a statement of the
quantity and type of goods required. It may take the form of
a letter, but usually it is on a printed form.

Where headings are printed (as in Fig. 24) the left-hand margin is set to coincide with the beginning of the heading. Usually this gives a left-hand margin of one inch (25 mm). The right-hand margin must not be wider than the left-hand margin.

Preparation of a memorandum form

Where printed memo forms are not available the memo is typed on A5 landscape paper (210 × 148 mm).

An example of a layout is shown in Fig. 25. Margins are set at 10 and 75 (pica) or 12 and 90 (elite). The message is typed in single-line spacing with double between paragraphs. The date ends at the right-hand margin. The starting point is obtained by back-spacing once for each character or space.

```
(Turn up 4 lines)

MEMORANDUM

(Turn up 4 lines)

FROM:  Miss S Bean                      DATE:   1 July 19--
(Turn up 2 lines)
TO:     Mr P James                      REF:    SB/HN
(Turn up 2 lines)
_____
(Turn up 2 lines)
Library Requisition
(Turn up 2 lines)
I should be grateful if you would let me have a list of books which
you would like to be added to the History section of the school
library.
```

Fig. 25 Layout for a typed memorandum form

ATTITUDE   A pleasant, smiling manner is far more appealing to visitors than a straight face. Similarly, a polite greeting is a more effective welcome than casual indifference.

APPEARANCE   Good grooming and a careful method of dress are important factors in creating a favourable impression on visitors.

SPEECH   Clear speech is essential in a job involving conversation with people face-to-face and over the telephone.

Shoulder headings

This type of heading is begun at the left-hand margin and may be in closed capitals. If it is typed in lower case with initial capitals, it must be underscored. It is separated from the material below by one blank line.

The difference between paragraph headings and shoulder headings should be noted. Whereas with paragraph headings the text begins on the same line as the heading, with shoulder headings the text starts on a separate line.

Example e

Type a copy of the following on A4 paper (210 × 297 mm), using indented paragraphs and single-line spacing. Centre the main heading on the typing line. Set margins at 12–72 (pica), 22–82 (elite).

<u>COMMERCE</u>

(Turn up 3 lines)

People who work in commercial occupations are engaged in assisting the movement of raw materials in industry and the distribution of finished goods from industry to consumers. There are several main groups of commercial occupations.

(Turn up 2 lines)

<u>TRADE</u>

(Turn up 2 lines)

Trade means buying and selling in either home or foreign markets. Thus people who work in the retail and wholesale trades, the import and export trades are commercial workers.

(Turn up 2 lines)

<u>TRANSPORT</u>

Transport by road, rail, sea and air distributes raw materials and finished goods to where they are required.

EXERCISES

Exercise 1

Type a memo on A5 landscape paper (210 × 148 mm) using the information given below. Turn up 4 lines from the top of the paper before typing the word MEMORANDUM. Use single-line spacing for the message. Set margins at 10 and 75 (pica) or 12 and 90 (elite).

```
From:  Headmaster

To:  Head of English Department

Subject:  STAFF MEETING

Today's date

A meeting will be held in the School Library on Thursday
afternoon at 4 o'clock.  Will you please inform the members of
your department and urge them to attend.
```

Exercise 2

Type a memo from Annette Rykel to Mr B Fieldman. The memo should be dated for 10 January 19––. Use A5 landscape paper (210 × 148 mm).

CHARISMA COSMETICS

stet
δ) I attach for yr consideration the 1st draft of a ~~new~~ publicity handout to ~~publicise~~ promote Charisma's latest range of skin care products.

run on (This will accompany the illustrations now being finalised ~~prepared~~ in the Art Dept.

δ) u.c. ~~A~~ separate ~~leaflet for~~ material in respect of the co-ordinating lipstick & nail varnish range ~~is in course of~~

δ) ~~preparation &~~ will be ready in time for the conference on 25 Jan. The overall size of this leaflet will be 30 cm x 21 cm.

(Y.R.E.B.)

Paragraph headings

A paragraph heading may be typed either in lower case with initial capital letters and underscoring or in closed capitals with or without the underscore. Paragraph headings may be followed by a punctuation mark or they may run on without punctuation.

Example c

Type a copy of the following on A5 landscape paper (210 × 148 mm) in single-line spacing in blocked style. Centre the main heading, using spaced capitals; for the sub-heading use lower case with initial capitals for each word and underscore. Set margins at 12–72 (pica), 22–82 (elite).

T H E   P O S T   O F F I C E

(Turn up 2 single lines)

Means of Payment

(Turn up 3 single lines)

Stamps. Postage stamps are sometimes used for small payments by post. The receiver can either use them himself or sell them back to the Post Office at a discount of 12½ per cent of the face value of the stamps.

Postal Orders are issued for varying sums. In addition to the amount of the order, poundage is charged. The purpose is to cover the cost to the Post Office of handling this form of payment.

Registered Post. Bank notes can be posted in a registered envelope and insured. A special registration fee is payable and when the envelope is posted a receipt is obtained from the Post Office.

Example d

Type a copy of the following on A5 landscape paper (210 × 148 mm) in single-line spacing with indented paragraphs. Centre the main heading, using spaced capitals; for the sub-heading use lower case with initial capitals for each word and underscore. Set margins at 12–72 (pica), 22–82 (elite).

Note   If, as here, a full stop is not used after the paragraph heading, three spaces should be left before starting the text.

R E C E P T I O N   W O R K

Personal Qualities

Particular attention should be given to the following factors by those who wish to be receptionists.

Exercise 3

Type on A5 landscape paper (210 × 148 mm).

From Purchasing Manager
To N R Brown
Ref BW/KG

<u>Recent Advertising Campaign</u>

NP

I enclose 18 forms completed by prospective clients who are living within your area. [Please follow through in the usual way.

Encs

(R.S.A.)

Exercise 4

Type on A5 landscape paper (210 × 148 mm).

From Superintendent   Ref MDC/RB/7
To   All Traffic Controllers Date

<u>Mediaeval Fair - Road Blocks</u>

Because of the alteration in the May Day programme which brings the May Queen Parade forward to 1100 hours, it will be necessary for road blocks to be erected at the strategic points previously outlined by 0900 hours. The restriction will remain in force until 1600 hrs.

(R.S.A.)

Example a

Type a copy of the following on A5 landscape paper (210 × 148 mm). Use blocked paragraphs and single-line spacing. Centre the main heading (using spaced capitals) and the sub-heading. Set margins at 12–72 (pica), 22–82 (elite).

P A Y M E N T   O F   T A X E S

(Turn up 2 single lines)

Personal Tax

(Turn up 3 single lines)

Wage-earners and salaried workers pay income tax by the pay-as-you-earn (PAYE) method. The amounts due are collected by the employer for the Inland Revenue before the employee receives his pay. The amount deducted from each pay packet depends on how much an employee has earned.

Some people do not pay personal tax by the PAYE method because the amount of money earned in a particular week or month is not known. For example, people who run businesses of their own work out their earnings on an annual basis.

Example b

Type a copy of the following on A5 landscape paper (210 × 148 mm). Use blocked paragraphs and single-line spacing. Use blocked style for the main heading and the sub-heading. Set margins at 12–72 (pica), 22–82 (elite).

THE TELEPHONE

Making calls

Telephone numbers can be looked up in a directory. Within an organisation the various extension numbers are contained in an internal directory. Subscribers to the national telephone system are listed in directories published by British Telecom.

The main types of directories include alphabetical directories and classified business directories. Alphabetical directories are published for different areas of the country and each directory lists the names, addresses and telephone numbers of subscribers in a given area. Classified business (Yellow Page) directories are useful for obtaining names and addresses of those engaged in a particular trade or profession.

108

Exercise 5

Type on A5 landscape (210 × 148 mm). Use today's date.

From   The Secretary   Ref   SCM/55

To   All Departments

Staff Club membership

At the Annual General Meeting of the Staff Club held on 24 June, it was agreed that retiring members of the staff would, provided they were members of the club at the time of their retirement, be eligible to be elected life members of the club on payment of a single fee of £2.50 and that no further subscriptions would be required of them.

Members of the staff who are also members of the club or approaching retirement are invited to apply for the appropriate form of application.

(R.S.A.)

Exercise 4

Display the following on A5 landscape paper (210 × 148 mm). Centre each line horizontally and the whole exercise vertically.

```
Closing Down Sale.  All prices reduced.
Jewellery, clocks, watches, gold and
silver items.  We must close on Saturday,
30 April.  Everything must be sold.
No reasonable offer refused.
Sid Sham the Jeweller, 1 Prison Road, Keepville.
```

Exercise 5

Display the following on A5 portrait paper (148 × 210 mm). Centre each line horizontally and the whole exercise vertically.

```
Motor Show Preview to be held in the
Diesel Hall at 10 30 am on 4 and 5 October.
Free admission by ticket only obtainable
from Mr F A N Belt, Sales Manager, Mighty
Motors Mart, Tyre Way, Oiltown.
```

24 Headings

Headings form an important part of display.

Main and sub-headings

A *main heading* (which gives the title or subject of a passage of writing) is typed in capital letters. If these are *spaced* capitals then one space is left between each letter. Three spaces are left between each word in spaced capitals.

A *sub-heading* appears directly under a main heading. Usually it is typed in lower case with initial capital letters and is underscored.

Main headings and sub-headings may be typed either in blocked form or centred over the line of typing.

19 Postcards

A postcard has a short message (which is not private) on one side and the address to which it is going on the other.

Many organisations have their name and address printed across the top of the side used for the message (Fig. 26). However, if the address has to be typed, it should begin at the left-hand margin. (Fig. 27)

There is no inside address, salutation or complimentary close on postcards.

Type the following exercises on postcards or if postcards are not available, use a sheet of A5 paper folded or cut into half pieces.

BELL & HYMAN LIMITED, *Publishers,* Denmark House, 37/39 Queen Elizabeth Street, London SE1 2QB
Telephones: 01-407 0709 and 01-407 5237   Cables: Bellhyman, London SE1

```
2 May 19--

Ref AF/NT


A First Course in Typing

Thank you for the list of alterations and
corrections.

A Forsyth
```

Fig. 26 Postcard with printed name and address

Selection of paper

If there are only a small number of lines in a display, but these are of considerable width, then *A5 landscape* is the best choice. On the other hand, when the display is longer but narrow in width (such as, for example, with a menu) then *A5 portrait* is the most suitable.

When a piece of display is too long to fit attractively on A5 portrait (50 lines of space from top to bottom), then A4 should be used (70 lines from top to bottom). The latter may be preferred, too, if a particular item requires a wide border of white space around it to make an attractive display.

EXERCISES

In each of the following exercises make a plan for displaying the material before starting to type.

Exercise 1

Display the following on A5 portrait paper (148 × 210 mm). Centre each line horizontally and the whole exercise vertically.

```
Universal Department Stores Limited require
part-time sales assistants in all departments
during December.  Apply in writing to Personnel
Officer, Universal Department Stores Limited,
Retail Road, Tradetown.
```

Exercise 2

Display the following on A5 landscape paper (210 × 148 mm). Centre each line horizontally and the whole exercise vertically.

```
Annual General Meeting of the Sweetmeadow
Country Club will be held on Tuesday,
9 March at 2 pm in the Tulip Hall.
All members are invited to attend.
```

Exercise 3

Display the following on A5 portrait paper (148 × 210 mm). Centre each line horizontally and the whole exercise vertically.

```
The Friends of Churchfold School.  Annual
Dinner will be held on 1 December at the
Hotshot Hall.  Reception 7 15 pm. Tickets
may be obtained from the Secretary,
Mr A Reck, 4 Schoolway Street, Grimtown.
```

```
(Turn up 5 lines)


CURTAINS LTD   12 High Street   NEWTOWN NE3 4WN
(Turn up 1 line)
_____

(Turn up 3 lines)

Date as Postmark
(Turn up 2 lines)
AL/NO

(Turn up 3 lines)

We are pleased to inform you that your
curtains are now awaiting collection.
(Turn up 2 lines)
Manager
```

Fig. 27 Postcard with typed name and address (side 1)

POST CARD

THE ADDRESS TO BE WRITTEN ON THIS SIDE

```
Mr A L Jones
193 South Street
WESTOWN
WE4 3WN
```

Fig. 28 Postcard with recipient's name and address (side 2)

23 Planned display work

When no guidance is given as to the method of display required, it is helpful to make a rough sketch showing how the material is to be arranged. Lines should be divided at natural points and prominence given to key features.

Example

The advertisement below is to be displayed on A5 landscape paper (210 × 148 mm).

```
Sunny Shore Guest House offers holiday accommodation.
Situated five minutes from the sea.  Good food and a warm,
friendly welcome.  Special catering for children.  Write for
brochure to John Merryman, Sunny Shore Guest House,
Seaville.
```

A plan can be pencilled on paper as follows:

Line 1 —————————— SUNNY SHORE GUEST HOUSE
①

Line 2 —————————— offers holiday accommodation
①

Line 3 —————————— situated five minutes from the sea
①

Line 4 —————————— Good food and a warm, friendly welcome
①

Line 5 —————————— Special catering for children
②

Line 6 —————————— Write for brochure to
①

Line 7 —————————— John Merryman
①

Line 8 —————————— Sunny Shore Guest House, Seaville

The figures in circles show lines of space.
Each line is centred horizontally and the whole advertisement vertically.

EXERCISES

On side 1 use margins of 1.25 cm (half an inch) and follow the spacing shown in Fig. 27. On the reverse side, type the address. Turn up half-way (14 single lines) before starting to type side 2. The same rules as for envelopes apply when typing the name and address to which the card is being sent.

Exercise 1

```
To:   Mammoth Enterprises Ltd   100 Commercial Way   RUSHTOWN
      RU4 6WN

From:   Colossus Combine Ltd   Trade House   Industry Road
        ROARVILLE   RO3 2LE

Ref AG/LO                       Today's date

Message:   Thank you for your letter of (insert date).

           This matter is receiving attention and I will
           write to you again shortly.

A Greatman
Branch Manager
```

Exercise 2

```
To: Mrs L A Simpson   12 Park Street   Birmingham   B17 9AM

From: Consumer Catalogues Ltd  9 Mail Order Road
      London WL3 60N

REF WT/PN                       Today's date

Message:   Thank you for your order received today.

           We regret that item number 2 is out of stock at
           present, but will be dispatched as soon as
           supplies are received.

W Temple
Sales Manager
```

Exercise 5

Display the following in blocked style on A5 portrait paper (148 × 210 mm).

BIRMINTON ADULT INSTITUTE

offers

EVENING CLASSES

in

Commerce
Economics
Accounts
Office Practice
Typewriting
Shorthand

ENROL NOW

Exercise 6

Display the following in blocked style on A5 portrait paper (148 × 210 mm).

LILYWHITE TENNIS CLUB

SEVENTY FIFTH ANNUAL DINNER

at the Crossed Nets Restaurant
Westbridge

on

Saturday 18 April

at 7 30 pm

Tickets £5.50 per person

Exercise 3

To: S R Tibbs Esq 2 Crab Court Crook Street
    Manchester MA2 8TO

From: Shady Motor Sales Ltd 4 Gearbox Close
      Manchester MA9 3PT

Ref SG/AB   Today's date

Message: We have pleasure in advising you that the set of
          wheels ordered by you is now to hand, and we await
          your instructions.

S Greaser
Parts Department

Exercise 4

To: Miss H R Thomas 12 Dancing Drive Wolverhampton WL4 3HN

From: The Twirl Shop 3 Points Road Wolverhampton WO1 6PT

Ref AT/PS   Date as Postmark

Message: We are pleased to inform you that the ballet shoes
          which you ordered have now arrived.

A Tapper
Manageress

Blocked display

This style of layout is an alternative to centred display. Instead of each line being centred across the page, the left margin is used as a common starting point.

Example

The following menu is to be displayed in blocked style on A5 portrait paper (148 × 210 mm).

```
MENU


Grapefruit

Roast Turkey
Chipolata Sausage
Cranberry Sauce
Roast and Creamed Potatoes
Garden Peas

Fruit Tart

Coffee
```

Vertical display

The material is arranged with equal top and bottom margins in the usual way.

Horizontal display

The longest line is centred across the page.
The left margin is set at the beginning of this line. All lines begin at this point.

Exercise 4

Display the menu given above in blocked style.

V DISPLAY

Display means the orderly and effective arrangement of material on a page.

20 Horizontal Display: equal margins

A first step in learning how to display is to understand how short lines are set out in the centre of the paper. This means arranging the material so that there is equal space on either side. The following steps are required.

(1)   Move margin stops to the extreme left and right.

(2)   Insert the paper with the left edge at 0 on the paper scale and read off the number of typing spaces at the right edge. This gives the total number of spaces from edge to edge of the paper. (Fig. 29)

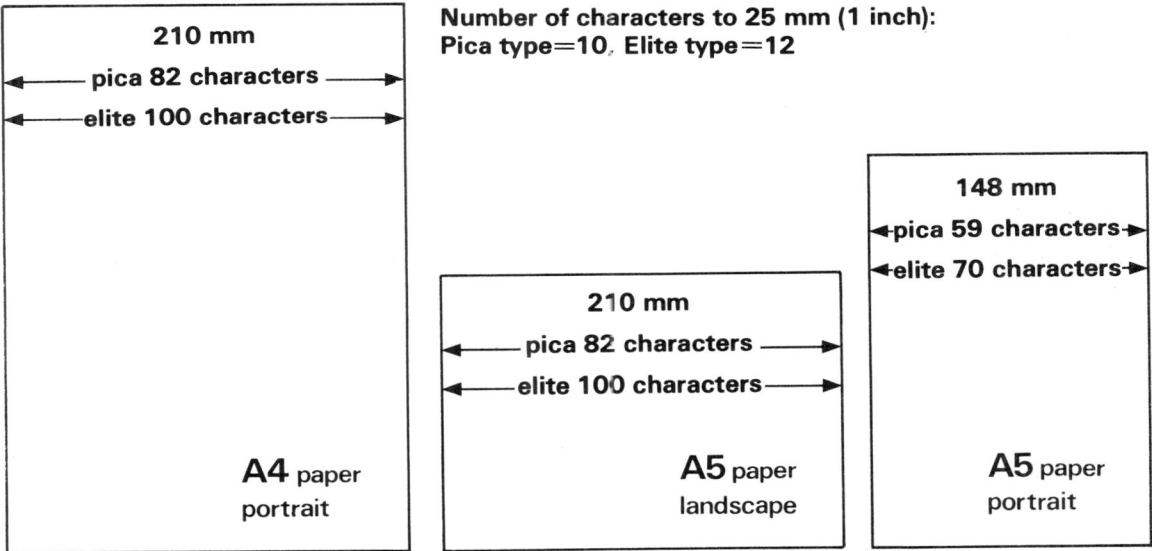

Fig. 29 Typing spaces

(3)   Halve this number to find the centre point of the paper.

(4)   Move the carriage until the printing point is at the centre of the page. Set a tab stop if centring more than one line.

(5)   Backspace once for every two letters or spaces in the line of typing.

In the example below there are 11 letters plus 1 space and so it is necessary to backspace 6 times. Any odd letter left over is ignored.

(6)   Begin the typing line from the point reached.

Exercise 2

Centre each line horizontally and the whole exercise vertically. Use A5 landscape paper (210 × 148 mm).

```
        SUNNY HILLS PRIMARY SCHOOL
        Parent-Teacher Association

                DINNER/DANCE

                to be held at

            THE BOLD FORESTER
          Oak Street, Deerham

             Reception 8 pm

        Dancing to the FRENETICS

                Tickets £2
```

Exercise 3

Centre each line horizontally and the whole exercise vertically. Use A5 portrait paper (148 × 210 mm).

```
          THE GOOD LIFE HOTEL


                  MENU


              Tomato Soup


        Roast Lamb - Mint Sauce
          New Boiled Potatoes
               Garden Peas


              Peach Sundae


                 Coffee
```

EXERCISES

Centre each of the following lines. Use double-line spacing.

Begin by moving the margin stops to the extreme left and right and ensure that the left edge of the paper is against the paper guide at 0.

Exercise 1

British Rail   (12 typing spaces)

The Top Twenty   (14   ”   ”   )

The Wizard of Oz   (16   ”   ”   )

The Stock Exchange   (18   ”   ”   )

Typewriting Room

The Sound of Music

The King and I

Oliver

Exercise 2

Disco Dancing

Kew Gardens

Top of the Pops

Coronation Street

Miss United Kingdom

City of London

Post Office

A Midsummer Night's Dream

(2)   Count the number of typing lines and blank lines in the material to be centred. In the example 10 typewritten lines plus 5 blank lines = 15 lines.

(3)   Deduct this total from the number of lines down the page. (35 − 15 = 20)

(4)   Divide the result by two to find out how many lines will appear equally above and below the material (20 ÷ 2 = 10). Any fraction is ignored.

(5)   Insert paper ensuring the left edge is at 0 on the paper scale and the top edge is level with the alignment scale.

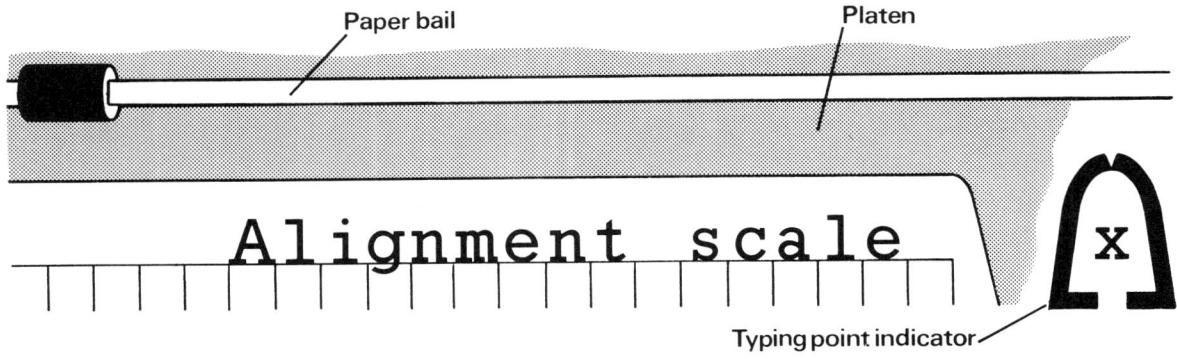

Fig. 31 Drawing to show alignment scale

(6)   Turn up the number of spaces calculated for the top margin (10) plus one extra space. Typing begins on line 11 in order to leave 10 clear lines from the top edge of the paper.

(7)   Type the display, centring each line horizontally. Turn up twice when it is necessary to leave one line of space.

EXERCISES

Exercise 1
Centre each line horizontally and the whole exercise vertically. Use A5 landscape paper (210 × 148 mm).

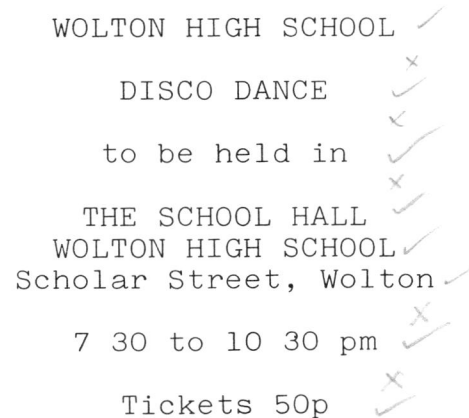

WOLTON HIGH SCHOOL

DISCO DANCE

to be held in

THE SCHOOL HALL
WOLTON HIGH SCHOOL
Scholar Street, Wolton

7 30 to 10 30 pm

Tickets 50p

Exercises 3 and 4

Type a copy of the following in double-line spacing on A5 portrait paper (148 × 210 mm). Centre each line horizontally. Turn up 18 single lines from the top of the paper.

Exercise 3

OFFICE JUNIOR

required for

busy City Office.

Apply by letter, as soon as possible, to

Office Manager

Bears to Peru Ltd.

Paddington Street,

London.

Exercise 4

AUCTION SALE

of

Domestic Appliances

at

23 South Street, Lowtown

on

12 and 13 January

2 pm to 4 30 pm

one in a hundred of these flowers develops into a cocoa pod.
Inside each pod there are from thirty to forty white beans
which do not turn cocoa-brown until they have been harvested
and allowed to ferment and dry.

(R.S.A. – part question)

22 Horizontal and vertical display

Vertical display means the arrangement of material on a page so that there are approximately the same number of blank lines left at the top and bottom.

Example

This advertisement is to be centred vertically on A5 landscape paper (210 × 148 mm).

```
            CHURCHFOLD HIGH SCHOOL
             (Turn up 2 single lines)
                   requires
             (Turn up 2 single lines)
                 EXPERIENCED
                  FULL-TIME
                  SECRETARY
             (Turn up 2 single lines)
                     also
             (Turn up 2 single lines)
               DINNER SUPERVISOR
             (Turn up 2 single lines)
             Apply in writing to
                The Headmaster
             Churchfold High School
```

The following steps are required.
(1) Find out the number of typing lines from the top to the bottom of the paper. (Fig. 30) On A5 landscape paper there are 35 lines.

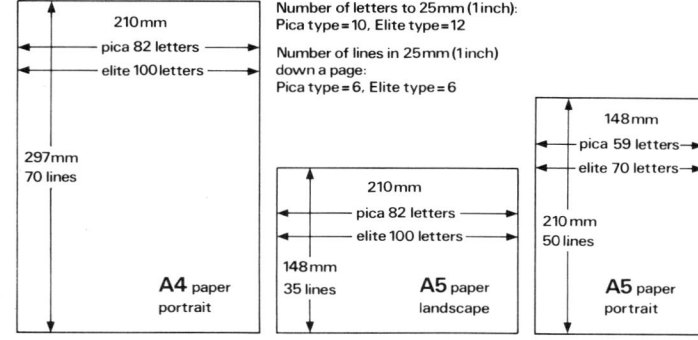

Fig. 30 Typing lines

Exercise 5

Type a copy of the following in double-line spacing on A5 portrait paper (148 × 210 mm). Centre each line horizontally. Turn up 17 single lines from the top edge of the paper.

```
                    FAIRFIELDS HIGH SCHOOL

                        SUMMERTOWN

                    SKI HOLIDAY TO AUSTRIA

                    Pre-Ski Fitness Classes

                            in

                       School Gymnasium

                    every Monday afternoon

                            at

                         3 45 pm
```

21 Horizontal Display: unequal margins

In addition to knowing how to centre material on the page, it is necessary to learn how to centre on the typing line. This means displaying material centrally when the page margins are not equal. The following steps are required.

(1)   Insert the paper with the left edge at 0 on the paper scale and set margin stops as required. E.g. left margin at 12 and right margin at 72.

(2)   Add together the points at which the margins are set and divide by 2 to find the centre point of the typing line. E.g. 12 + 72 = 84 ÷ 2 = 42 centre point.

(3)   Bring the carriage to the centre point and backspace once for every two letters or spaces in the line of typing. An odd letter is ignored.

(4)   Begin the typing line from the point reached.

Exercise 5

Type the following exercise on A5 landscape paper (210 × 148 mm) in single-line spacing. Set margins at 12 and 72 (pica), 22 and 82 (elite). Turn up 14 lines from the top edge of the paper.

A Basic Commodity   → centre
(Turn up 2 single lines)

      Oil is believed to have originated from the action of microbes upon the bodies of tiny sea-creatures in the absence of air. Oil can, therefore, be present only in strata which have been formed below the sea.

run on   Together with the crude petroleum two other materials occur, namely, natural gas above it and salt water below. It is the business of the petroleum geologist to locate these underground structures and to suggest the sites for wells so that the oil will be struck rather than the GAS or
caps   SALT WATER.

      The petroleum industry comprises the production of crude oil, the transport of the crude oil to a refinery and its manufacture there into a range of joint products.

(R.S.A. – part question)

Exercise 6

Type on A4 paper (210 × 297 mm). Use double-line spacing and indented paragraphs. Set margins at 12 and 72 (pica), 22 and 82 (elite). Leave a space of 22 single lines from the top edge of the paper.

A TIN OF COCOA   → centre
(Turn up 3 single lines)

caps   In 1877, a west african blacksmith named Tette Quesi travelled from Fernando Poo back home to the Gold Coast and with him he carried a single cocoa pod containing about thirty beans. The beans were planted and one grew in the course of a few years into a cocoa-bearing tree.

      The cocoa tree is rather like an apple tree in size and shape. It has broad dark-green leaves. On the trunk itself and on the lower leafless parts of the main branches there grow thousands of delicate pale blossoms. Only about

EXERCISES

Exercise 1

Type a copy of the following on A5 landscape paper (210 × 148 mm), using blocked style and double-line spacing. Centre the heading over the typing line. Set margins at 12 and 72 (pica), and 22 and 82 (elite). Turn up 13 lines from the top edge of the paper.

SCHOOL RULES

(Turn up 3 single lines)

Parents on behalf of their children undertake to maintain the rules and regulations of the School. The reputation of the school owes much to the loyal support of parents who have co-operated in keeping up standards of behaviour and discipline.

Exercise 2

Type a copy of the following on A5 landscape paper (210 × 148 mm), using indented style and single-line spacing. Centre the heading over the typing line. Set margins at 15 and 70 (pica), and 25 and 80 (elite). Turn up 13 lines from the top edge of the paper.

BUSINESS STUDIES CERTIFICATE

(Turn up 2 single lines)

The examination leading to awards may be taken at any age. The following sections will comprise the examination: (a) Communications, (b) Background to Business, (c) Office Practice, (d) Audio Typewriting OR Shorthand Typewriting.

Exercise 3

Type a copy of the following on A5 landscape paper (210 × 148 mm), using blocked style and double-line spacing. Centre the heading over the typing line. Set margins at 12 and 72 (pica), and 22 and 82 (elite). Turn up 13 lines from the top edge of the paper.

THE QUESTION OF DEFROSTING

(Turn up 3 single lines)

Defrosting is completely automatic in the refrigerator cabinet. The defrost water drains out to the back of the cabinet where it evaporates. The freezer is not automatically defrosted. Frost should be removed at intervals. It should be done when there is little or no frozen food in the freezer.

Exercise 4

Type a copy of the following on A5 landscape paper (210 × 148 mm), using indented style and double-line spacing. Centre the heading over the typing line. Set margins at 12 and 72 (pica), and 22 and 82 (elite). Turn up 11 lines from the top edge of the paper.

THE PREMIER HOTEL

(Turn up 3 single lines)

This hotel offers a glorious welcome to the south. Each suite has its own patio, with a magnificent view of the surrounding countryside. Every one of the 215 bedrooms is fully equipped to modern luxury standards.